I0796787

Praise for Manifest Like a Witch

'Lilly Statham is a manifestation queen, sharing her witchy gifts to create spells, charms, and potions to supercharge your manifesting goals. This book is literally "practical magic"! Manifest Like a Witch *is a must-read book for anyone wanting to take back their power and actively create an abundant life in the most wonderfully witchy way.'*

KAREN KAY, author of *Fairy Whispering*

'A beautifully practical and empowering guide for any witch ready to stop waiting and start creating. This book is like a warm coven hug wrapped in spell jars and candlelight. Whether you're just beginning or returning to your magic, Manifest Like a Witch *will remind you that you are powerful, worthy, and more than capable of conjuring the life you dream of.'*

EMMA GRIFFIN, author of *The Witch's Way Home*

'In this book, Lilly Statham offers practical yet potent spells you can create with everyday items – a perfect reminder that the most powerful magic often starts right at home.'

YASMIN BOLAND, bestselling author of *Moonology*™

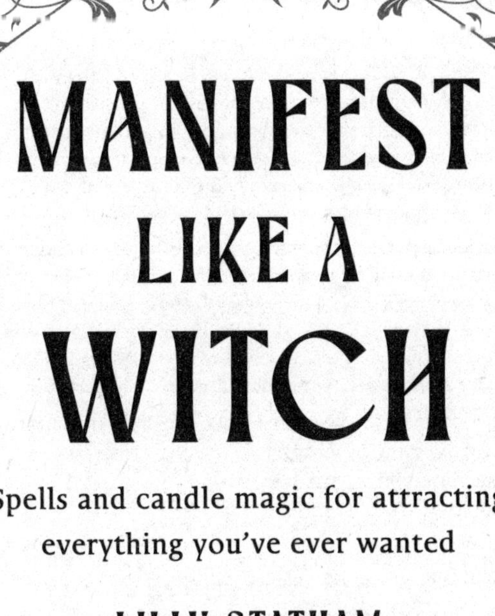

MANIFEST LIKE A WITCH

Spells and candle magic for attracting everything you've ever wanted

LILLY STATHAM
Founder of Mystic Primrose

HAY HOUSE
Carlsbad, California • New York City
London • Sydney • New Delhi

Published in the United States by:
Hay House LLC, www.hayhouse.com®
P.O. Box 5100, Carlsbad, CA, 92018-5100

A catalogue record for this book is available from the British Library.

Hardcover ISBN: 978-1-4019-9902-5
E-book ISBN: 978-1-83782-580-6
Audiobook ISBN: 978-1-83782-578-3

1st Printing

Printed in the United States of America

This product uses responsibly sourced papers, including recycled materials and materials from other controlled sources.

The authorized representative in the EU for product safety and compliance is Penguin Random House Ireland, Morrison Chambers, 32 Nassau Street, Dublin D02 YH68, Ireland. https://eu-contact.penguin.ie

I am dedicating this book to every witch who has been, and will be, in hope that they will manifest their dream life using the power of witchcraft. Magick resides in all of us, we just need to remember to tap into it.

CONTENTS

Introduction
1

A homage to our witchy ancestors
3

Trust the magick
4

Types of spellwork
6

Spice up your spellwork
13

Preparing, casting, and closing
16

Spell safety and ethics
29

Free will in magick
30

Spells

Manifest Focus, Flow, and Fulfillment

Get motivated candle spell
37

Clarity and focus spell jar
40

Sail through any interview candle spell
43

Level up your career candle spell
46

Travel new roads candle spell
49

Find your voice candle spell
52

Good luck spell jar
55

Overcome challenges charm bag
58

Start that new project candle spell
61

Be the best at what you do spell jar
64

Grow your followers charm bag
67

Ease your workload spell jar
70

Manifest a Life of Abundance

Quick cash candle spell
75

Money bowl
77

Pay rise candle spell
81

Banish debts candle spell
84

Financial freedom spell
87

Get paid what you're owed candle spell
90

Dream house spell jar
93

Manifest a successful business spell jar
96

Manifest that special item spell jar
100

Trip of a lifetime abundance bowl
103

Manifest Your Inner Magick

Confidence booster candle spell
109

Happiness and positivity candle spell
112

Inner strength candle spell
115

Call your power back candle spell
118

Open your third eye candle spell
121

Raise your energy candle spell
124

Align with your highest self spell jar
127

Shadow work spell jar
130

Divine feminine energy candle spell
133

Divine masculine energy candle spell
136

Self-love spell jar
139

Manifest Healthier Relationships

Find your true love candle spell
145

Manifest new friendships spell jar
148

Reconciliation candle spell
152

Get your ex back spell jar
155

Get noticed candle spell
158

Spice up your sex life candle spell
161

Protect your relationship spell jar
165

Let go and move on cord-cutting spell
168

Cool down tempers candle spell
171

Reinforce your boundaries candle spell
174

Strengthen your bond candle spell
177

Heal a broken heart spell jar
180

Manifest Protection and Peace

Self-protection spell jar
187

Pet protection spell jar
191

Protect your loved ones candle spell
195

Banish hexes and curses fire spell
198

Protection from the evil eye spell jar
202

Return-to-sender candle spell
205

Reveal the truth spell jar
208

Banishing burnout candle spell
212

Get a good night's sleep spell jar
215

Put your mind at ease candle spell
218

Keep safe on the move spell jar
221

Additional Recipes, Tools, and Charts

Black salt
226

Moon water
228

Money rice
230

How to create sigils
232
Correspondence Charts
234
Herbs and spices
234
Candle colors
236
Crystals
237
Runes
239
Reading your candle flames
242
Timings
244

A Final Note
247
Acknowledgments
249
About the Author
251

INTRODUCTION

Firstly, I just want to congratulate you for opting to open this spell book! You've made a smart choice. I'm assuming by picking up this book you're done with living a mediocre life and are now ready to step into the world of witchcraft and manifest your dream life. I don't blame you; this is exactly how I felt before I started on my witchcraft journey. It's safe to say witchcraft has utterly changed my entire life for the better and now I want to help you do the same.

If you're just starting out on your witchcraft journey, my own personal grimoire (aka this book) is here to show you that witchcraft isn't scary and just the simplest of manifestations and rituals will change your life. If you're already a well-oiled machine when it comes to witchcraft, you'll still find something in these pages to spark fresh ideas, offer a new perspective, or inspire your next ritual.

In today's busy society we're often thinking of a million things at once and running around like crazy to get everything done. I expect the last thing on your mind is finding the time to squeeze in witchcraft and perform long lengthy rituals. But rest assured, practicing witchcraft doesn't have to take hours out of your life – you can often manifest your deepest desires while on the go. Simply sprinkling cinnamon in your coffee will help you to manifest more abundance in your life (more on that later).

The spellwork you're going to find in this book isn't comprised of complicated incantations and rituals that feel inaccessible and leave you confused; it includes simple yet powerful spells that can be created from the materials that you likely already have in your house. Worst-case scenario, I'll be sending you to your closest grocery store to pick up a lemon or two. But that's it. My aim is to show you that you already have the power within you to manifest whatever you want in life. All you need is a little insight and direction on how to do so, and this is where I come into play!

Being able to harness the power of manifestation through witchcraft *will* change your life. So, what is it? Manifesting through the power of witchcraft is the practice of using your intentions, along with magickal tools, and aligning your energy to turn your dreams into reality. It blends the philosophies of universal manifestation lore, such as belief and visualization, with traditional witchcraft practices like spellwork, herbs, crystals, and moon magick. In other words, it's *the* most powerful way to manifest whatever the hell you want. Whether that's your dream home or ideal career, manifesting like a witch will get you there. So, sit back, grab your coffee, and get ready for me to take you on the witchcraft trip of your life!

A homage to our witchy ancestors

Before we start, I think it's only right that we pay homage to our witchy ancestors – after all, they taught us everything we know today. You may be the first witch of the family that you know of, but I'm sure somewhere down that very long line there was another witchy relative who started in the same position that you're in right now. Witchy blood runs through our veins; we just need to learn to tap into it.

Witchcraft can officially be traced all the way back to the 10th century, but let's be honest, it has more than likely been around even longer than that. Many cultures across the world incorporated witchcraft into their lives in one way or another; from the ancient Egyptians, who used spells and amulets for protection and healing, to the Vikings, who employed *seiðr* – a form of Norse magick – for divination, spirit communication, and influencing fate.

Over time, I'm sure we're all aware that witchcraft gained a bad reputation, particularly as religious institutions gained power and witches became associated with heresy, devil worship, and moral corruption. This shift led to fear, persecution, and witch hunts, often targeting women and marginalized individuals. Now I'm not saying all witchcraft is good, as I'm pretty sure there's a handful of witches out there who aren't scared of karma and are hexing to their hearts' content, but the majority of us use witchcraft for good intentions.

Before embarking on your own witchcraft journey, I think it's important to take a moment to pause and reflect on where we came from, to honor the witches who came before us – those who were misunderstood, persecuted, and even executed during the witch trials, and those who, against all odds, survived and kept the old ways alive in secret. They endured fear, isolation, and injustice simply for practicing what, to many of us now, is a path of healing, intuition, and connection. Taking a moment to acknowledge their struggles and resilience is not only an act of respect, but also a way of grounding your practice in history and gratitude.

Trust the magick: how it really works

Now some say magick and witchcraft is just *spicy* psychology or that it simply doesn't exist. There may be an element of spicy psychology at play here, but it's safe to say magick does exist. Whether it's science we just don't understand yet, or something else entirely, one thing for certain is that it's had a huge impact on society, shaping spiritual practices, influencing approaches to medicine and healing, and weaving its way through art and literature. Hollywood and pop culture have drilled into our heads that magick only exists in the form of green skin and black pointy hats, but in fact its psychological roots run much deeper.

The majority of spells and witchcraft all work in similar ways. They do so through intention, focused energy, ritualistic practices, and symbolic meaning. This combination allows us to tap into a perceived universal energy to manifest desired outcomes, with the belief that the very act of casting the spell itself can influence the desired result; essentially, it's the power of belief put into action.

At the root of all spellwork is manifestation – the ability to turn wants and desires into reality through the power of believing in yourself and the purposeful actions you take to achieve your goals. If you want something badly enough, you'll find a way to achieve it.

There are a variety of manifestation techniques, such as affirmations, vision boards, and meditation, all of which will help you to achieve what you want. As much as I love all these practices, spellwork has to be my favorite. Well, if you've seen my social media accounts it's obvious, right? All I do is preach witchcraft and how you can use it to get whatever you want.

To get the most from this book, you need to wholeheartedly trust in yourself and the universe. You have what it takes to manifest everything you desire – you just need a little faith and confidence in yourself to make sure you get there. You already are *that witch*; you just need to start believing it! As you turn these pages, remember: Magick is already within you, all you need is the courage to claim it. Let's manifest your dream life together – one spell at a time. So, grab a candle and gather your herbs; your magickal journey awaits…

Types of spellwork

There are many different types of spellwork within witchcraft, and therefore endless ways you can manifest whatever you want. Whether that be casting spells inside corked jars, lighting candles, or blending herbs together as if you're in Professor Snape's potion class. Some methods may suit certain intentions better than others. So, let's figure out which kind of spellwork best matches what you're looking to manifest.

Candle magick (aka fire magick)

Casting spells using candles is a simple and easy way to manifest what you want quickly and with power. With the potent energy from the fire and the ability to match your candle color with your intention, candle magick is a great way to get straight to the point without much fussing around. Depending on what you're wanting to manifest, big or small, you can match your candle size with your intentions. For example, if you're just looking to manifest a quick $100, you can simply use a small tea light to do so. However, if you're looking to manifest a bigger, steadier flow of money into your life, a large 100-hour candle would be perfect. This way you can light it each day for an hour at a time, over a 100-day period.

A candle spell in a nutshell

Candle magick is a very versatile way of manifesting your goals and often takes less than an hour to do (depending on the size of your candle), but the principles for each candle ritual remain the same.

Once you've decided on your intentions, you can pick a colored candle that aligns perfectly with them. For example, green is great for prosperity whereas pink is great for mending friendships *(see correspondence chart on pages 236-37)*. Although if you're in a hurry and don't have a chance to pick up a specific-colored candle, you can always opt for white. A white candle can represent any color and therefore will match with any intentions. You might be thinking, *Then what's the point in using colored candles in the first place?* Well,I find that colored candles make it easier to channel and focus on your intentions, rather than sitting there having to imagine your white candle is a different color.

After deciding on your candle color, you can then choose the herbs to use in your spell. You can specifically go out of your way to order in particular herbs, but in most cases you'll more than likely have a herb or spice lying around in your kitchen that will match your intentions (*see correspondence chart on pages 234-36*). Once you've selected your ingredients, there are a few different ways you can incorporate them into your candle spell. One way is to blend the herbs together, add a little oil (any type will do), and roll your candle in the herb mixture. Another way is to sprinkle the herbs around the base of your candle, either aesthetically or just by chucking them on. It's entirely up to you – witchcraft doesn't have to look glamorous and well put together. It's your intentions that matter.

Once you have your candle prepped, you're ready to set it ablaze. Well, just the wick! If you're feeling a little extra and want to add more to your spellwork, you can tie a piece of paper that you've written your intentions on to the candle and add some matching crystals (*see correspondence chart on page 237*). You can then carry these crystals around with you after the ritual to further cement your intentions.

As you light the candle, all you have to do is concentrate on your intentions and what you want to gain from this ritual. Now you can spend time meditating as the candle burns. Alternatively, providing you have left it in a *safe place* where nothing is going to catch fire, you can leave the room – just not the house! If you don't have the time to sit while your candle burns fully, you can turn it into a daily ritual. For example, if you're manifesting a lot of money, you can light the candle for seven days (7 = money in numerology) for seven minutes at 7:00 p.m. The time, the length of burning, and the number of days you take is entirely up to you. But make sure you burn the candle *fully* to ensure your spell is complete.

Spell jars

My personal favorite! Spell jars are a great way to manifest your intentions while on the go. Each spell jar can be made up of a variety of different ingredients, such as herbs, crystals, and handwritten notes, that all align perfectly with your intentions. When life is chaotic and you're in a rush, your spell jar excels. You simply add all your spell ingredients and seal them inside the glass jar. Now you can carry your manifestations and spellwork throughout your busy day-to-day life, continuing to work with your spell while getting on with all your important, more mundane tasks. It's as easy as that! Spells involving goal manifesting, protection, and love all go great inside a spell jar.

Spell jar basics

Much like candle magick, spell jars are extremely accessible and versatile. The principle to spell-jar making is to layer herbs and crystals that correspond with what you want to manifest in a glass jar *(see correspondence charts on pages 234-38)*. Alongside this, you should add in handwritten intentions and intentionally select the wax color you use to seal the jar. Spell jars can be used for a whole heap of different things, whether that's manifesting your dream home, or acting as protection wards for your house.

Spell jars have more longevity than other spell types, so you can carry on working with them for as long as you need. For example, you can create a money spell jar that will continue to be effective for years to come, as long as you work with it on a regular basis.

Now, what do I mean by working with it? There are a variety of different ways to do this:

Meditate: Meditating can help you to get crystal clear on your manifestations. As you meditate, focus on the intentions of your spell jar and channel your energy into it. This will charge your spell jar and help to remind the universe of what you're trying to manifest. You can meditate with it as often or as little as you like, but doing so regularly allows the energy of your manifestation to keep flowing.

Find the perfect place: The placement of your spell jar is important – keeping it in an area that aligns with your purpose is a great idea. Let's say you're trying to manifest a promotion at your current workplace. If your spell jar is at home in a dark corner, it's not going to work as well as if you were to place it on your office desk or take it to work with you. Keeping your spell jar in the area that aligns with your intentions also acts as a reminder to constantly work toward your goals and that your manifestations are on the way. After all, the universe needs to see that you want it! Not that you're just going to ask for something and then throw the spell jar in a corner and forget about it… because, let's be honest, do you really want it that much if you're not going to do much else about it? To ensure the best and quickest results, working with and being 'glued' to your spell jar is by far the better option.

Incorporate your spell jar into your rituals: You can use your spell jar within other rituals and spellwork. It's not a one-time tool; think of it as a battery for your intentions. For example, if you've created a money spell jar, you can use it as an anchor in any spells that relate to money… think of it as a power source for every money spell that you cast. You can also write down updates or observations relating to your spell jar's intentions and place them under or near the jar. This will help to keep your intentions alive, and your spell jar will continue to act as a beacon to draw in your manifestations.

Pair your spell jar with your divination practices. For example, if you want to know how your manifestations are coming along, place your spell jar next to your tarot or oracle cards while you're doing a reading. This can offer insights into what you need to do to speed up your manifestations. After the reading, tuck a drawn card or a sigil (*see page 232*) under the jar to reinforce guidance or outcomes.

The more time and energy you put into your spell jar, the more it gives back. Carry it with you, place it under your pillow each night, meditate with it, use it in other rituals… The deeper your connection to the spell jar, the easier your manifestations will come into your life. Think of your spell jar as your new best friend.

As with all types of spellwork, you can adapt your spell jars and candles to your needs. What works for one witch might not work for another. Choosing and creating your own path is always the best way to master your craft.

Herbal magick

This is when I feel like I'm a true alchemist, mixing and brewing potions to tend to my ever-growing needs. Blending herbs to create different types of herbal magick is the epitome of fun! Herbs can be used in a variety of ways, such as in herbal teas, cleansing potions, and charm bags. You can even take a regular old cup of joe, simply mix a little bit of cinnamon and nutmeg together, sprinkle it into your coffee and you're left sitting with a powerful elixir that will help draw in money and prosperity from the moment it touches your lips. Herbal magick pairs beautifully with both candle magick and spell jars – the herb mixtures you create can be sprinkled over your candles or inside your spell jars, making your spellwork that little bit more powerful and intentional.

Spice up your spellwork

There are plenty of ways to level up your spellwork. The following additions can help focus your energy, strengthen your intentions, and boost your manifestations.

Sigils

Creating sigils involves turning intentions into physical and practical symbols that can be used alone or woven through your spellwork to enhance the potency of your spells. Sigils are commonly created by writing down your intention, condensing the letters, and then creating a monogram out of what's left. Sigils are a very personal form of spellwork, as more often than not only the creator understands what the sigil represents. Sigils could be crafted for any kind of written intention. Examples include: 'I am more confident and happy within myself as each day passes' or 'I am protected against all things bad luck, evil, and harmful.'

Sigils can be written anywhere, whether that's a piece of paper you carry around with you every day, the steamed-up shower door, or even on yourself with a pen (body- and skin-safe pens only please!). Sigils are both extremely personal and powerful to the practitioner. Don't worry, I'll show you how to create one later in the book (*see page 232*) – either keep reading or skip to it right now if you must!

Runes

Another powerful tool to enhance your spellwork, runes have been used for centuries as a form of divination and magickal symbolism. Each rune carries its own unique meaning and energy, and can be used to cast spells, gain insight, or boost your manifestations. Unlike sigils, which you create yourself, runes come from an existing alphabet – most commonly the Elder Futhark – and each symbol taps into ancient energies tied to protection, clarity, strength, and so on (*see the chart on pages 239-40*). You can pull a single rune for guidance, carve one into a candle, or draw them onto objects or paper to weave into your spellwork.

Divination

The most fun part of witchcraft if you ask me – uncovering truths and finding out about the unknown. Divination can come in a variety of different forms, whether that's good old-fashioned tarot card reading, pendulum swinging, or something a little more 'exotic' such as candle wax scrying, which involves dripping melted wax into water and interpreting the shapes or symbols formed to gain insight or guidance. Using the power of divination while casting your spells is a great way to gain insight into the progression and success of your spellwork.

Now divination isn't necessary to ensure successful spellwork, but, my gosh, can it help! For example, using a pendulum is a great way to decide which tools and ingredients to use for your spellwork. Torn between two different herbs? Use the pendulum to decipher which will be more advantageous for that particular spell. The easiest way to use your pendulum is by asking yes/no questions. Take a moment to sit still, hold the pendulum steady in your hand, then ask it which direction is 'yes' and which way is 'no.' Give the pendulum a moment to start swinging while making sure your hand remains steady. Once you have your directions, you can then ask the pendulum your yes/no questions, and sure enough it will give you the answer.

Need a little intuitive guidance before casting your spell? Sit down with your chosen divination tool and spend a minute or two seeking guidance and clarity on the best way to approach your casting. For example, you can draw a tarot or oracle card from your deck to set the tone for your ritual and give you an insight into what you may need to ensure the spell is a success. By integrating divination, you'll ensure your spell is well-informed and in sync with the greater energetic flow. This practice deepens your connection to your intuition and the spiritual realm.

Words of affirmation

Using words of affirmation during your spellwork can help you home in on your intentions and bring direction and clarity to your spells. I've included some sample words of affirmation with each spell throughout the book, but you're more than welcome to adapt them to what feels right for you. Spontaneously saying whatever comes to mind during your spellwork is a great indicator of what you really want to manifest. These affirmations can be repeated as often or as little as you like. For example, if you meditate with your spell jar on a regular basis, you can repeat your words of affirmation to recharge it. This can either be out loud or in your head – it will work the same. Your witchcraft journey is yours and yours only, so adapt and tailor these affirmations to your needs. There's no set rule book for witchcraft, just go with your gut!

Preparing, casting, and closing: the whole shebang

Right, now down to the real magick and ensuring you get the most from your spells. Don't worry if you don't get it completely spot on the first time around – after all, witchcraft is a lifetime journey. You'll get better the more your practice and as time goes on. However, there's nothing wrong with getting a few insider tips from a well-seasoned witch to ensure you hit the ground running.

Preparation: mental and physical

Let's get the easiest bit out of the way: the physical preparation. Make sure you have all your ingredients and tools to hand before you cast the spell. It will save you hunting around your house mid-cast and breaking your flow. As you're getting ready to start manifesting whatever your heart desires, make sure you're in a quiet space where you won't be interrupted. There's no point in casting spells if you have people talking loudly in the background or people coming in and out of your space. If you're in a busy home, there's nothing wrong with casting your spell in the bathroom where there's a lock on the door.

Now the slightly more difficult part: mental preparation. I'm probably making this sound a little more scary than it actually is, but basically, all I'm trying to say is there's no point casting a spell mid-breakdown because you've just found out your ex is a cheating prick. You'll end up casting a spell with too many raw emotions, and the likelihood of it being a success is relatively slim. Make sure you're casting a spell from a calm and grounded place, even if you're casting a banishing spell for your cheating ex.

You'll be at your most powerful when you have a calm and steady mindset. Navigating your spell with a clear mind will ensure your intentions are at their strongest. Now, I'm not saying you should be happy after finding out your ex has been cheating on you; what I'm saying is of course you can be pissed off and hurt – I would be – but casting with a calm mindset will be a lot more beneficial and less likely to backfire than if you're doing spellwork with your hands shaking and tears streaming down your face.

Meditating and having a cleansing shower is a great way to get 'in the zone' before starting any spell. Also, top secret of mine: Playing a Viking mediation playlist really sets the mystical mood!

Pick the right ingredients and tools

The ingredients you use in your spellwork are essential – after all, without them, there's no spell to cast. Matching your herbs, crystals, and candle colors with your intentions is a great way to add power to any casting (*see correspondence charts on pages 234-38*). It allows you to channel the energy of your spellwork in the right direction. There's no point adding in a random ingredient that doesn't have any relation to what you want to manifest, because the universe is going to be like, 'What's this random bit of sugar doing in a banishment spell? I thought she wanted to banish her ex not attract them.' Take a few moments before each spell to pick out ingredients that you know will help amplify your intentions around what you're wanting to manifest. For example, if you're casting a love spell, then a red candle, rose petals, and rose quartz are the perfect corresponding ingredients.

Tools are similar to your ingredients, in that choosing the right tools for your intentions is a great way of focusing and channeling your energy. For example, placing your intentions and ingredients into a spell jar makes your spell portable, so you can carry it with you and manifest on the go. This is perfect if you're trying to achieve a particular set of goals within a specific time frame, or you simply want to continue manifesting while you're going about your day-to-day life.

Perfect timing

While timing, in my opinion, isn't an essential component of casting, it's a great way to add extra oomph to any spell. For example, if you're looking to let go of unwanted aspects of your life, casting your spell during a waning moon phase is perfect. Alternatively, you can time your spellwork with the Sabbats, the seasonal festivals that mark key moments in nature's cycle, such as Imbolc for new beginnings, Beltane for love and fertility, or Samhain for letting go. It's entirely up to you.

But you definitely don't have to wait a whole month or however long until the next appropriate moon phase. You can simply cast as soon as you feel called to do so, or pick a particular day of the week. Each day corresponds with different spell castings, for example, Thursday is a great day for money spells. A timing guide can be found at the back of this book on pages 244-46. I want to make witchcraft as easy as possible for you!

Intention, intention, intention

The most important part of spell casting is setting clear and concise intentions. Articulating clearly what you want to manifest or gain from your spell is imperative to its success.

This means getting down to the nitty gritty and writing out the specifics of what you want to achieve. This doesn't have to be difficult and complicated – if anything, the more straightforward the better. For example, 'I will manifest £1,000 in the next 60 days via Facebook reels bonuses' or 'I am going to move into my dream house located in the perfect area this year.'

Without specific intentions, your spellwork will lack direction and manifesting will be harder as you don't necessarily know where your energy is going. Fundamentally, your intentions will be the thing that ensures your spells are successful. Here are a few important things to consider when setting intentions for your spellwork.

Banish self-doubt

When it comes to manifesting what you want, you need to get rid of ideas like, 'I don't deserve it' or 'I'm not good enough.' We will have none of that negative attitude, thank you very much! Because guess what, you *do* deserve it, and you *are* good enough. Having self-doubt will act as a massive block when it comes to your spellwork – you're essentially telling the universe you want something, but you're not ready to receive it. And therefore, funnily enough, the universe will take longer to send it your way.

'How do I banish self-doubt?' you may ask. Well, it's not as difficult as you might think. Here are a few easy steps to take:

1. **Explore where the self-doubt is coming from.** Reflect on the real reason why you lack confidence. Ask yourself: Is it fear of doing the spell wrong? Are you worried that it won't work? That you're not 'powerful' enough? Being able to pinpoint these answers will allow you to address your negative thoughts directly. Once you know what's holding you back, you can begin to reframe your thinking. For example, if you're worried your spell won't work, shift the thought to, *If it doesn't work this time, I'll learn from it and try again*. If you feel you're not powerful enough, tell yourself, *My power grows every time I trust myself.* By acknowledging and challenging these doubts you strip them of their power and strengthen your self-belief.

2. **Redefine what successful spellwork looks like**. Spellwork isn't about fireworks or immediate results. It's about intention, alignment, and trusting in yourself and the process. You don't need special powers – you just need to be present and believe in yourself. Remember, a successful spell isn't measured by how quickly something manifests, and the magick often unfolds gradually; it may show up in unexpected ways or take time to fully take shape.

3. **Stop comparing yourself to other witches.** Like all witches, you're on your own unique path, and what works for someone else may not work for you. So, if you're doing spellwork that's slightly different to someone else, it doesn't

mean you're doing it wrong. The moment you honor your unique practice, self-doubt loses its grip.

4. **Practice, practice, practice!** Doubt shrinks with repetition. The more you cast, the more you realize *you* are the magick. When you see that your spells are working, your self-doubt will begin to disappear. It's so simple – do the spells, watch the results, and your self-doubt will be banished; it's a spell in itself!

5. **Use journaling as integration.** After any spell or casting, write down what you did, how it felt, and what thoughts came up. This isn't for critique, it's for connection. You'll see patterns emerge and start trusting your own rhythm. As you start to notice patterns of self-doubt, you can then find ways to resolve them. Here are a couple of journal prompts: *What would my spellwork look like if I trusted myself fully? How would I speak, move, and cast? What am I afraid will happen if I do trust my power fully? What if that fear is just the last illusion to clear?*

Focus your thoughts

Another way to ensure you manifest successfully is to remove any scattered thoughts when it comes to your intentions. Imagine this: You're ringing up the universe to ask for $10,000 in your bank account, but your mind is whirring and you're thinking of 101 different things. On the other end of the phone, the universe is sitting there listening to you waffle on about all these different things and isn't going to hear the part where you're asking for money, so it's going to have no idea why you rang or what you actually want.

Therefore, before each spell casting session, you need to clear out all the white noise and thoughts you've had throughout the day and concentrate solely on what you want. This way, when you 'pick up the phone' to the universe, it will hear your exact message asking for $10,000 in your bank account. A simple way to do this is to take a moment to write down all your scattered thoughts, then put them to one side while you carry out your spellwork. Alternatively, spend a few minutes meditating, getting in the zone. This will help clear your mind so you can focus on the intention of your spell. All those buzzing thoughts will be waiting for you afterwards – deal with them then.

Align your energy

To ensure your intentions are clear, you need to start aligning with and embodying the energy you want to manifest. There's no point trying to manifest a rich and abundant lifestyle if you're sitting at home bed-rotting, thinking about how poor you are, and doing nothing to change it. The universe must see that you're working toward what you want to manifest. If you're not making any efforts to reach your goal, and you're just sitting there waiting for it, the likelihood of the universe saying, 'You know what, they deserve this lifestyle so I'm just going to hand it to them' is very slim. The universe is probably thinking, 'I'm not going to give this lazy witch anything.'

So, it's all well and good casting a spell for your dream car but if you're not actively working toward receiving it then – news flash – it probably won't happen. For example, if your dream car is a Ferrari, start acting as though your current car *is* the Ferrari. Yes, it might not look like one, but in your mind and in your soul whenever you're driving it or sitting in it, you *are* driving a Ferrari, not the shit box you currently own. It's this kind of embodiment that will align your energy with what you're trying to achieve. And one day I promise it will be an actual Ferrari you're sitting in. You just need to keep working toward getting it, instead of sitting there and waiting for someone to drop one off on your doorstep. You need to take action yourself!

To use another example, it's all well and good casting a spell to find your one true love, but if you never leave the house, you won't find them – after all, the likelihood of your delivery person being the person you're looking for is pretty slim! Go to places where your person will be likely to turn up; take action toward your goal by actively seeking them out. This will, without a doubt, speed up your manifestations. There's no point sitting on your ass waiting for a miracle to make you happy. The universe needs to see you working toward your goals and only then will it send your desires your way.

Setting the scene for your spellwork

Casting spells in a chaotic environment is never going to give you the best results. So, before you start casting away, I recommend setting up a designated space to do your work where you won't be interrupted. This could either be an entire room dedicated to your witchcraft, or you could simply set up a tranquil spot within your bedroom where you can concentrate on your intentions and not get distracted. It doesn't need to be anything big and fancy, but having an area where you can focus on your intentions and a place to put your spell workings is a great start. In other words, create a witchy altar. How do you do this? Let me give you a quick run-down.

An altar doesn't have to be set up in a particular way, as each witches' altar is unique to them, but here are some things you can include to create your own personal spell casting space:

- A table or sturdy surface
- An altar cloth – witchcraft can get messy!
- A pestle and mortar for mixing up magick blends
- Ambient lighting (turn off the big light!) – this could be candles, fairy lights, you name it
- A few of your favorite personal trinkets and crystals

- A handy little box or cupboard where you can store some essential spell supplies – plates, a lighter or matches, candles, string, glass jars and containers, herbs and spices, black salt (*see page 226*), and moon water (*see page 228*)
- A fireproof dish or cauldron
- An athame, used to direct energy, cast circles, or cut energetic cords
- A mirror, to use in ancestor work, shadow work, or communicating with guides
- A Book of Shadows, to document your journey and spell findings
- Incense, to cleanse your space and your energy
- A candle holder

While you don't need all these things straight away, having a few bits and pieces is always a good idea. A sacred space like an altar doesn't have to be finished within the first week, it can be something that evolves over time alongside your practice. So don't worry about getting all the equipment right away, just pick up pieces here and there when you can.

Now for the fun part... casting the spell!

During your spell casting, as we've discussed, the best thing you can do is focus on your intentions in an environment free from distractions. As I outlined earlier, focusing solely on your intention while performing your ritual is the key to success. At the same time as speaking your affirmations (out loud or in your head), visualize the universe sending your manifestations your way. Let go of any doubts you may have and trust in the process. And more importantly, trust in yourself and your own powers.

There's no rule saying how long your spell should take; it could take 10 minutes or it could take an hour. As long as you're 'in the zone,' that's all that matters. Your spell will naturally come to a close when the time is right. At this point, take a moment to ground yourself and show gratitude toward the universe for listening to your wants or needs. Finally, make a note of your spell and any thoughts or feelings that arose during the casting (preferably in your Book of Shadows). You don't have to do this straight away – leave it a day or two if necessary.

Once you've successfully cast your spell, there are a couple of things to remember to further secure its success. The main thing being patience. Spells take time to manifest. Trust the process and avoid obsessing over the results. Also, don't be afraid to repeat your spell multiple times. Repetition and consistency are great ways to strengthen your connection with your intentions and your craft. And finally, making your spells your own, by following my spell guides but putting your own spin on them, is a great way to increase the effectiveness of your craft. Embrace the beauty of spellwork as a journey, not just a destination. With each spell, you're not only manifesting your goals but also deepening your connection to the energy that flows through you and the world.

Discarding of spellwork

Once you've cast your spells, you may be sitting there wondering what the hell to do with what's left. Well, in a nutshell it's entirely up to you. But let's say your spell jar has done its job and you no longer have any use for it, here's how you can dispose of it:

First, empty the spell jar of its contents; anything biodegradable can go in the compost heap or be returned to the earth; anything reusable, such as the jar itself, can be cleaned and used again (you can pick off any wax and the cork should still be intact); and anything that can't be reused you can just throw in the trash. With regards to candle magick, it's a similar process – reuse what you can, bury the biodegradable stuff, and throw out what's left. It's as simple as that.

Spell safety and ethics

Just before we get on to the spells themselves, it's important that we quickly run through the ethics of spellwork. Ethics within witchcraft aren't necessarily rules, but act as a framework for practitioners to ensure they behave with grace and integrity. Conducting spells in the right manner and for the right reasons is very important. Magick is manipulating energy and tapping into many different spiritual realms, so ensuring it's done correctly and safely is imperative.

Spellwork can have energetic impacts on yourself and others. Using spells for personal growth, healing, and manifestation is primarily what witchcraft is for. However, there are those who use spellwork for the harm or manipulation of others – but these people who use witchcraft for evil intentions take the risk of running with karma herself. Using magick to harm, manipulate, or seek revenge is not only ethically questionable but can also backfire energetically. Many traditions believe that negative intentions return to the caster, magnified.

Here's a list of basic ethics to bear in mind when manifesting through spells:

- It's best practice to ask for permission before casting a spell for someone else, even if it's for their benefit.
- Avoid spells that could harm or manipulate others, even unintentionally.

- Magick is a tool and not a weapon – it should be used for your own personal goals and to better the lives of those around you.

- Magick is most powerful when used to uplift, empower, and align with the greater good. For example, a prosperity spell to attract opportunities rather than take wealth from others, or a self-love spell to enhance confidence rather than forcing someone else's affection.

Free will in magick

Free will is essential in witchcraft and shouldn't be overlooked. Magick is a tool for empowerment, but use it while respecting others. Interfering with free will goes against a person's ability to consent and therefore can have unintended energetic and karmic consequences to the spell caster. Take this as me warning you not to interfere with someone's free will as it may come back to bite you on your ass!

Everyone has a right to make their own decisions without external interference (i.e. you!). Now this isn't to say you can't cast spells for others or that may impact others, just make sure there's goodwill behind your intentions. For example, if you want your ex back (I know how it feels), make sure your intentions are that you want them to come back only if a part of them also wants to do so. Magick is there to uplift and empower you and others rather than coerce and control. Attempting to override free will can disrupt and alter the balance of energy and may result in negative repercussions for the witch. Trust me, karma exists… so hear my warning, witches! Many spiritual traditions believe in the 'Rule of Three' or similar karmic laws, where the energy you put out returns to you threefold. So just be careful, as you'll reap what you sow.

As the Wiccan Rede states, 'An' it harm none, do what ye will.' In other words, if your intentions do no harm, do whatever the hell you want! Then again, if you're not worried about the Wiccan Rede, or you're like 'darn the consequences,' go for it! But just be prepared for what might be heading your way as a result. I do stress being a good witch is very important both ethically and for your own well-being.

Energetic imbalances created by controlling magick can ripple through relationships and environments, creating more harm than good. I've learnt from my mistakes, so when I say it's not worth it, trust me it's not. A good example is love spells. We've all been there, desperately wishing for someone back, even when it feels beyond impossible. But casting a spell to force someone back almost always ends in tears. I myself made that mistake once, and will certainly never be doing it again. From one witch to another, it is *not* worth it, despite how badly you feel like you need them. Instead, you can cast a spell to open the road to reconciliation and what is meant to be, rather than forcing someone back against their free will. Alternatively, casting a spell to find your perfect partner naturally is a great idea!

Now the part you've all been waiting for: the spells! If you've just skipped to this section looking for a 'Get your ex back' spell, you're in luck, but I highly recommend you go back and read through my points above, so when it comes to casting your spell it's a success. Because if you come to me saying your spells don't work… I'll say, 'Did you read the introduction first?'

SPELLS

Now let's get on with manifesting your dream life like a true witch. The following spells are ones that I've used over my 15 years of practicing witchcraft, all of which have worked perfectly for me. Think of them as a snippet from my own personal Book of Shadows. You're welcome!

Remember before each spell to set the scene (*see page 25*). To help me get in the right frame of mind, I like to make myself comfortable at my altar. I turn off the big light, light a few candles and some incense, and put on my favorite Viking-themed meditation playlist. Some of my go-to artists for this are Heilung, Warduna, and Eivor. I find doing these few things beforehand helps clear my mind so that I can focus solely on my intentions. It also makes the ritual seem a little more magickal and witchy than if I were to rush in without any preparation.

MANIFEST FOCUS, FLOW, AND FULFILLMENT

At times, finding the energy and motivation for everyday life can be a challenge – let alone staying driven to advance your career. That's where I find this set of spells comes in handy. Included are spells to increase your productivity, boost your motivation, manifest your dream job, and embark on new journeys. They're designed to lighten your load and provide a much-needed boost in the areas you feel it most. They will help clear the path to success, making it all feel just a little more effortless. It's time to level up in life, unleash your inner boss energy, and get that bag!

Get motivated candle spell

Right, let's start off with an easy one – after all, if you're looking for a motivation spell the likelihood of you wanting a complex lengthy ritual is slim to none. This simple candle spell is designed to reignite your motivation while providing you with a boost of energy that will allow you to get the job done.

What you'll need:

- A white candle (for mental clarity and energy clearing)
- Coffee granules (to give you that little energy boost)
- Salt (to get rid of that pesky procrastination)
- Lemon juice (to remove brain fog and provide you with the drive you need)
- A candle holder
- A lighter or matches

What to do:

1. **Set the mood:** Find a place where you won't be interrupted. This is your time to focus on clearing your mind and getting your shit together. After all, you have a whole to-do list to get through but zero energy. Turn off the big light, switch on your fairy lights, and take a moment to yourself.

2. **Clear the negativity:** Take a deep breath, let go of any negativity, and mentally brush off any energy that's not serving your highest self. Visualize all that heaviness leaving your headspace as you exhale.

3. **Get intentional:** Hold that white candle like it's your key to getting your whole life back on track. Now say this affirmation like you mean it:

   'I'm calling on motivation and drive. I let go of all things that are holding me back from working at my full potential. The universe is working in my favor, to get things done. So be it.'

4. **Light it up:** Place the candle in a candle holder, set the wick ablaze, and watch the flame work its magick. Focus on your intentions and know that with each flicker, you're drawing in motivation and drive.

5. **Add a little spice:** Take your coffee and salt and sprinkle them around your white candle. It's these ingredients that

will remove your need to procrastinate and provide you with the energy you need to get shit done. Now squeeze a little lemon juice onto the candle (avoiding the flame) and surrounding salt and coffee. This will give you that 'wide awake feeling' so you're ready to get things done.

6. **Let it burn:** As the candle burns, visualize your energy increasing and your motivation levels soaring.

Witch Tip

Perform this ritual at your desk or the place where you need to do your work. As the candle burns carry on working and ticking off those tasks. If you're not at home and don't feel comfortable performing a witchy ritual in your office, perform it in the morning just before you go to work.

✦ ✦ ✦

Clarity and focus spell jar

Being able to sit down and fully concentrate on what you need to do can be difficult when you're thinking of a million-and-one other things. It also doesn't help when brain fog clouds your direction, preventing you from getting clear on the next steps you need to take. This spell jar is designed to help you get laser focused on the matter at hand as well as provide the clarity needed to get the job done. Perfect if you're easily distracted.

What you'll need:

- A corked glass jar
- Water or moon water (*see recipe on page 228*)
- Dried lavender (to relax your brain so that you can focus on what's at hand)
- Ground turmeric (to get those brain cogs working)
- Dried rosemary (for concentration and focus)
- Salt (to remove any blockages and provide mental clarity)

- A white candle (to seal in your intentions)
- A lighter or matches

What to do:

1. **Cleanse the jar**: Before you start throwing things into the jar, make sure it's squeaky clean. This way any residing energies that may affect your spell will be removed. A simple run under the tap will do but for extra witchy vibes, cleanse with moon water.

2. **Clear your mind:** Take a moment to clear and calm your mind. Concentrate on the task at hand and try not to think of anything else. This will help to quieten your internal chatter and bring clarity to your situation.

3. **Get intentional:** Sprinkle the lavender, turmeric, rosemary, and salt into your spell jar while saying the following:

   'My mind is sharp. My thoughts are aligned. I see the path ahead with perfect clarity.'

4. **Seal in the power:** Now it's time to seal in your intentions. Pop the cork lid on your jar then light your candle and drip the melted wax over your lid, binding your spell jar shut. You can use as much or as little of the wax as you like. Just make sure the lid won't pop off.

5. **Boost the energies:** Now that you've finished making your spell jar, spend five minutes holding it in your hands while focusing on your intentions. This acts as a final boost that charges your spell jar with your intentions. Then place it in an appropriate area where you'll see it often. For example, if you need help focusing on finishing an assignment, keep it on your desk.

Sail through any interview candle spell

Do you have an important interview coming up that you can't afford to mess up? Don't worry, I've got you covered! Let's make sure you sail through it, impress your interviewers, and land that dream job. After all, they'll have no reason not to hire you once you've done this spell.

What you'll need:

- Dried basil (for prosperity and abundance)
- Dried peppermint (to sharpen the mind and improve communication)
- Dried thyme (for courage and success in new endeavors)
- A green candle (for good luck and success)
- A plate
- Oil (any cooking oil will do)

+ A business card from the business where you're trying to get a job
+ A lighter or matches

What to do:

1. **Set the mood:** Find a place where you won't be interrupted. This is your moment to focus on clearing your mind and any doubts you may have about your interview. It's time to get super serious and sure of yourself, knowing that this interview will be a success.
2. **Mix your herbs:** Start by mixing your basil, peppermint, and thyme together, all the while thinking about the fact that you're going to breeze through your interview with ease.
3. **Dress your candle:** Next, grab your green candle and lie it across your plate. Drizzle the oil over your candle then sprinkle over your herby mixture. Roll the candle in the herbs until it's fully covered, always picturing yourself receiving an offer for the job you're being interviewed for as you do this.
4. **Light it up:** Place the business card on the center of your plate. Then melt the base of your candle (just hold it over a lighter for a few seconds) and stick it upright on top of

the business card. As you're visualizing your successful interview, set the wick ablaze and watch the flame work its magick. Focus on your intentions and know that with each flicker, you're drawing in success and the new job.

5. **Let it burn:** Spend a moment thinking about your successful interview, and say the following:

   'I am confident, capable, and prepared. My words flow with ease, my mind stays sharp, and success is already mine. The perfect opportunity aligns with me now.'

   Allow the candle to burn fully, then put the remains into a little bag and take it with you to the interview.

6. **Finish up:** Once you've completed your spell, it's time to sit back and relax ahead of the big day. The hard work has been done – all you have to do now is turn up to the interview. You already know that you're going to nail it, so do your best, be confident, and smash it out of the park. Good luck!

Witch Tip

Perform this ritual the night before your interview.

✦ ✦ ✦

Level up your career candle spell

Ready to take your career to the next level? Of course you are! This spell is designed to support your professional growth and help you step onto the next rung of your career ladder. Whether you're aiming for a promotion in your current role or calling in a more aligned position elsewhere, this spell is going to get you there.

What you'll need:

+ A gold candle (for growth and success)
+ Ground cinnamon (for prosperity and abundance)
+ Oil (any cooking oil will do)
+ Pen and paper
+ A plate
+ A lighter or matches

What to do:

1. **Visualize your success:** Find a place where you won't be interrupted. This is your time to focus on leveling up your career. You deserve it! Set down all your ingredients and get in the mindset to manifest what you want.

2. **Dress your candle:** Start by grabbing your gold candle and cinnamon. I want you to cover that candle in cinnamon – don't go too overboard with it, but make sure it's completely covered in a nice thin layer. Use a little oil to help the cinnamon stick to the candle. This will give your gold candle even more of an abundance boost.

3. **Get intentional:** Next, put your candle to the side and take a moment to really think about what you want to manifest. A promotion within your current workplace or a new job that's more aligned with your career vision? Visualize what your life is like as though you already have it. Get really specific on what you want and write it down. For example:

   'I have just received a promotion for the company I currently work for. They have given me a new position with a great job title and excellent perks.'

4. **Light it up:** Place the manifestation note on the plate. Then melt the base of your candle (just hold it over a lighter for a few seconds) to stick it on top of the note you've written.

As you're visualizing your life having already received the promotion, set fire to the wick. Watch the flame work its magick. Focus on your intentions and know that with each flicker, you're drawing in success.

5. **Let it burn:** As your candle burns, think about your leveled-up career, and say the following:

   'I am worthy of success, and my hard work is recognized and rewarded. Opportunities flow effortlessly to me, and I am stepping into my next level of achievement. The promotion I desire is already mine.'

   Once the candle has burnt fully, blow any remains to the wind, making sure you're focusing on your intentions the entire time.

6. **Let it go:** Once you've completed your spell, it's time to sit back and relax. You've sent your message to the universe, now all you have to do is patiently wait and the promotion will come to you.

Travel new roads candle spell

Looking to embark on a new journey? Whether that's traveling along a different career path, finding a route to improve your financial situation, or a journey of personal growth, this spell is designed to remove any blockages that may prevent you from reaching new horizons. It will clear any stagnant energy, break through limitations, and invite in new possibilities. Sounds exciting, right? So, let's get on with it.

What you'll need:

- An orange candle (for opportunity and movement)
- Ground cinnamon (for prosperity and abundance)
- Ground ginger (for momentum and driving energy forward)
- Dried peppermint (to refresh energy, remove stagnation, and attract new opportunities)
- Oil (any cooking oil will do)

- Bay leaf (for clarification and banishing unwanted blockages)
- A pen
- A plate

What to do:

1. **Visualize your path ahead:** Find a place where you won't be interrupted. This is your time to focus on removing anything that's blocking your path to success. I want you to spend a few moments really visualizing the new opportunities you want to come your way. This could be a new career, the chance to make more money, to travel the world, literally anything. Make sure your vision is crystal clear. The clearer your vision, the easier the path will show itself to you.

2. **Dress your candle:** Cover the candle in a good layer of each of your herbs and spices. This will give your candle the magick needed to get those new doors opened. If you want your ingredients to stick a little better to the candle, add a tiny bit of oil before you sprinkle them on.

3. **Get intentional:** Next, put your candle to the side for now and take a moment to get really clear about what you want to manifest. What doors would you like to be opened and why? What roads do you want to travel along? Get really

specific and visualize what your life is like as though you're already on your desired path. While doing so, draw a simple road on your bay leaf.

4. **Light it up:** Place the bay leaf on the plate. Then melt the base of your candle (just hold it over a lighter for a few seconds) to stick it on top of the leaf. Light the candle and say the following:

    'I clear the road before me, removing all blocks and barriers. Opportunities flow to me with ease and doors open in my favor. I welcome success, abundance, and new beginnings. The universe supports my journey, and I step forward with confidence and clarity. My way is open, my path is clear, and I am ready to receive all that is meant for me. So it is.'

5. **Let it burn:** As your candle burns, think about your new roads ahead and what opportunities they're going to bring. Once the candle has burnt fully, blow any remains to the wind, making sure you're focusing on your intentions the entire time.

6. **Sit back and relax:** Your new opportunities are on their way! It's just a matter of time.

Find your voice candle spell

Ever felt unable to formulate a cohesive sentence, let alone a speech, because your nerves have taken over? Yup, we've all been there, whether it's an important meeting, a difficult conversation with a partner, or a nail-biting presentation. Well, I've crafted this spell to help with just these sorts of situations. You'll be speaking like a TED talk pro before you know it!

What you'll need:

- A blue candle (for communication)
- Ground cinnamon (for confidence and good luck)
- Oil (any cooking oil will do)
- Pen and paper
- A plate
- A lighter or matches

What to do:

1. **Set the mood:** Find a place where you won't be interrupted. It's time to focus on finding your inner voice so that you can speak confidently and eloquently in all situations. After all, you already know what to say, you just need the confidence to do so. Set down all your ingredients and get in the mindset to manifest what you want.

2. **Dress your candle:** Start by grabbing your blue candle and cinnamon. Completely cover the candle in a thin layer of the cinnamon and use a drizzle of oil to help it stick. This will give your spell even more of a vocal boost.

3. **Get intentional:** Next, put your candle to the side and take a moment to focus on your manifestations. What parts of communication do you need divine help with? Getting your feelings across? Remembering lines? Write down whatever comes to mind. Get really specific, for example:

   'I have the courage to speak my truth.
   I release any fear and doubt. I trust my words
   to vocalize with clarity and power.'

   Then visualize what life is like having found your voice. Imagine it already so. How does it feel to speak confidently? What doors does it open? How do people treat you now?

4. **Light it up:** Place your manifestation note on the plate. Then melt the base of your candle (just hold it over a lighter for a few seconds) to stick it on top of the note. Visualize your voice magnifying and your confidence beginning to radiate, and watch the flame work its magick. Focus on your intentions and know that with each flicker, you're drawing in a newfound voice.

5. **Let it burn:** As your candle burns, spend a moment thinking about your leveled-up communication skills. Once the candle has burnt fully, blow any remains to the wind. Focus on your intentions the entire time.

6. **Let it go:** Once you've completed your spell, it's time to sit back and relax. You have sent your message to the universe, now all you have to do is patiently wait and your confident voice will come to you.

Good luck spell jar

In need of a little good luck? Feel as though it's just one piece of bad luck after another? Fear not, I'm here to be your little lucky leprechaun. Well not really, but I am here to help you get back your lucky streak.

What you'll need:

- A corked glass jar
- Moon water (*see recipe on page 228*) or an incense stick
- A lighter or matches
- Dried basil (the ultimate good luck herb)
- Cinnamon stick (for bringing in success and prosperity)
- Rose petals (for continuous joy and happiness)
- Salt (for protection against any bad luck)
- Bay leaf (for success)
- A green candle (for good luck)

What to do:

1. **Cleanse the jar:** Let's remove all the dust and residing energies in that glass jar to ensure it's squeaky clean and ready to make you the luckiest person alive! Simply wash it out using your ready-made moon water (or cleanse using an incense stick), dry it off, and you're ready to go!

2. **Mindfully add your ingredients:** Once your jar is clean, layer in the herbs, rose petals, and salt. As you add them (it doesn't matter the order) concentrate on each ingredient's properties. For example, as you're adding cinnamon to the jar, focus on bringing in fast success and prosperity. With each ingredient added, you're drawing in more good luck.

3. **Seal in the power:** After filling your spell jar, pop the cork lid on then light your candle and drip the melted wax over the lid, sealing your spell. You can repeat affirmations such as:

   'I attract good luck in every moment. The universe brings me what I need with ease. I am open, ready, and I welcome every lucky break meant for me.'

4. **Keep the jar in a place of power:** Place your spell jar in an area where you're confident it will bring you the most amount of luck. This could be the front entrance to your

home, on your desk, underneath your pillow… Just go with your gut instinct.

Witch Tip

Shake your jar occasionally to activate its energy or simply meditate with it whenever you have the chance. This will ensure you'll continue getting closer to your dream.

✦ ✦ ✦

Overcome challenges charm bag

When you face challenges that get in the way of pursuing your goals, it can be overwhelming and sometimes it feels like burying your head in the sand is the easiest option. But let's be honest, these problems won't go away, and ignoring them will just make you even more stressed in the long run. Learning to face obstacles as they come along will help you to become more resilient. Even now as you're reading this, I can imagine that you're thinking about a seemingly impossible challenge that's blocking your path forward. Well, what if I told you I had a spell to make it easier for you? Because I do, and here it is! So, go and grab your herbs because whatever challenge you're facing is about to become a distant memory.

What you'll need:

- A little organza bag
- An incense stick
- A lighter or matches
- Pen and paper

- Ground ginger (for a boost of courage)
- Dried chili (to repel any self-doubt)
- Dried mugwort (to enhance your inner vision)
- A bay leaf (for clarification and banishing unwanted blockages)
- A piece of string

What to do:

1. **Cleanse the pouch:** Before you start throwing things into the organza bag, make sure it's squeaky clean. We don't need any negative energies affecting your mindset. Simply grab an incense stick, light it, and wave it in and around your bag to neutralize its energies.

2. **Get intentional:** Take a moment to write down your goals. Make them short and sweet – this way you'll have true clarity on what you're aiming for rather than a wishy-washy meandering list.

3. **Fold in threes:** Once you've written your intentions on your piece of paper, fold the paper three times, toward you. With each fold, turn the piece of paper 45 degrees clockwise. This clockwise motion is great when you're trying to bring something into your life. Then pop the paper into the bag.

4. **Mindfully add your ingredients:** It's now time to add in the rest of your ingredients. It doesn't matter what order they go in, just focus on each of the ingredient's properties as you add them. For example, 'May this ginger give me the courage and confidence to overcome this challenge with ease.'

5. **Seal in the power:** Next, seal in your intentions. Grab your piece of string and wrap it around the top of your bag, tying it securely so that none of your ingredients and intentions spill out.

6. **Charge it:** Now that you've finished making your charm bag, spend five minutes holding it in your hands while focusing on your intentions. This acts as a final boost that charges your bag with your intentions. Then carry this little pouch with you wherever you go to act as a reminder that you're bigger and better than this challenge and nothing can stop you from reaching your goals.

Witch Tip

Before adding your bay leaf, draw the Tiwaz rune (*see page 241*) on it with a marker to gain extra strength and the willpower to push through your challenges.

✦ ✦ ✦

Start that new project candle spell

We all have projects and hustles we want to start but continuously put off, either because we don't think we'll be able to make them work, or they seem monumentally massive and we don't know where to begin. What if I told you that the new project you have in mind is your key to getting closer to manifesting your dream life? Whether that's starting a new business or engaging in a hobby you've always wanted to try, this spell will help you to get started with ease. So, go and grab the ingredients listed down below and let's get this new project started – no more procrastination, just action and enjoyment!

What you'll need:

- A bowl of water (to wash away any negative energies holding you back)
- A cinnamon stick (for passion and momentum)
- Dried peppermint (to clear mental fog and awaken your senses to take initiative)
- A piece of paper with your name on it

- A tea light
- A lighter or matches

What to do:

1. **Set the mood:** Take a moment to find a quiet spot where you won't be distracted. Press play on your favorite meditation playlist and take a few deep breaths. Allow any stress to disappear with each exhale. It's time to get excited for this new project – it's going to be sooo worth it!

2. **Combine your ingredients:** Next, sprinkle your peppermint into the bowl of water then add the cinnamon stick and the piece of paper with your name on it (you only need a small amount of water in the bowl; don't fill it completely). The minty water surrounding your name will clear away any negative doubts you may have about your project.

3. **Light it up:** Place the tea light in the bowl on top of your name. Make sure the water doesn't cover your candle or you won't be able to light it. The candle symbolizes the energy you need to kick-start your passion project. Set that candle alight!

4. **Visualize success:** Allow yourself time to sit with the candle and focus on what you want to create. Visualize yourself

starting the project and realizing how much enjoyment you're getting from it. Get excited!

5. **Take action:** When you're ready, blow out the candle and visualize your action plan starting to take place. Empty the bowl of water down the drain and get started on your project. I'm excited for you!

Alternative: You could always make this into a lovely herbal tea to sip on each morning. Just don't add the paper or tea light – I can't imagine that would taste too nice!

Witch Tip

While casting your spell, place a piece of carnelian into the water for extra confidence and courage to start this new project. Carry on with the spell as stated above but once you've finished, keep the carnelian as a reminder of your passion for this project.

✦ ✦ ✦

Be the best at what you do spell jar

Whether you're a personal trainer, a lawyer, or a professional witch, this spell is designed to help you become top tier within your field. Whatever area you're looking to excel in – your career, creative work, business, or spiritual practice – this spell will give you the ultimate confidence boost, the recognition you deserve, and will align you with your highest potential.

What you'll need:

- A corked glass jar
- An incense stick
- A lighter or matches
- Dried basil (for success, prosperity, respect, and to enhance your natural talent)
- Cloves (for recognition and attention)
- Dried peppermint (for success and good luck when in company of your competition)
- Ground cinnamon (for success and magnetic energy)

- Pen and paper
- A yellow candle (for success and confidence)

What to do:

1. **Cleanse your mind and jar:** Let's remove all your worries and self-doubt. Grab an incense stick, light it, and swirl it around yourself and your glass jar. Take a moment to relax your mind and focus on becoming the best at what you do.

2. **Mindfully add your ingredients:** Once your vision and intentions are clear, take a moment to add your herbs into your jar. As you add each ingredient (it doesn't matter the order) visualize being the best person in your field. Imagine it already so – no one can compete with you! Think in detail about how excited, proud, and confident you feel now that you're getting the recognition you deserve. Soak it up!

3. **Get intentional:** Once all your ingredients have been added, write down on your piece of paper your name and the field you're in. Something along the lines of:

   'My name is___ and I am the world's leading expert in___.'

   Then fold your paper toward you three times to symbolize bringing your intentions closer to you. With each fold, turn the piece of paper 45 degrees clockwise. This clockwise

motion is great when you're trying to bring something into your life. Add the paper to your jar.

4. **Seal in the power:** After filling your spell jar, pop the cork lid on. Light your candle and drip melted wax from it over the lid, sealing your spell.

5. **Charge it:** Now that your jar is complete, spend a few minutes getting crystal clear on your intentions and say the following affirmation:

   'I am wildly talented, deeply focused, and fully aligned with my purpose. I rise with power, lead with confidence, and attract success with ease. I am the best at what I do – and the world recognizes my magic. Nothing can stop me.'

6. **Place with purpose:** Put your spell jar somewhere you'll see it on a regular basis, or even better, carry it with you wherever you go as a constant reminder that *you are the best*. I know it, you know it, and now so does the rest of the world. Embody it!

Grow your followers charm bag

In this day and age, the more followers you have on your social media platforms, the more opportunities it brings, whether that's fame, brand deals, orders, or new connections. Growing your social media is a great way to bring in new and exciting opportunities, and this spell will ensure the algorithms are working in your favor. Before we start, a quick warning: This doesn't mean you can post and ghost – you still need to put in the work. *However*, it will make the whole process that much easier.

What you'll need:

+ A little organza bag
+ An incense stick
+ A lighter or matches
+ Pen and paper
+ Dried basil (for success, prosperity, and loyal followers)
+ Catnip (for magnetic energy to draw people in)

- Rose petals (for charm, beauty, and attracting positive attention)
- Calendula (for visibility, public success, and warmth)
- Sea salt (for clearing blocks, inviting good vibes, and clarity of message)
- A piece of string

What to do:

1. **Cleanse the pouch:** Before you start throwing things into the bag, make sure it's squeaky clean. Simply grab hold of an incense stick, light it, and wave it in and around your bag. This will neutralize any energies it's carrying.

2. **Get intentional:** Take a moment to write down your social media usernames and the goals you're trying to achieve. A specific follower count, views, you name it… write it down. This will ensure the universe knows which social media accounts you want to grow.

3. **Fold in threes:** Once you've written your names and intentions on your piece of paper, fold the paper three times, toward you. With each fold, turn the piece of paper 45 degrees clockwise. This clockwise motion is great when you're trying to bring something into your life. Then pop the paper into the bag.

4. **Mindfully add your ingredients:** Now add in the herbs and salt. It doesn't matter what order they go in, just focus on each of the ingredient's properties as you add them. For example, 'May this calendula provide me with visibility and public success.'

5. **Seal in the power:** Next it's time to seal in your intentions. Grab your piece of string and wrap it around the top of your bag, tying it securely so that none of your ingredients and intentions spill out.

6. **Charge it:** Now that you've finished making your spell bag, spend five minutes holding it in your hands and focusing on your intentions. This acts as a final boost that charges your bag with your intentions. Then carry this little pouch with you wherever you go to act as a reminder to post on your platforms and find ways to help them grow.

Witch Tip

As you're editing your social media posts, draw the Wunjo rune (*see page 240*) somewhere within your content and turn the opacity levels to zero. This way you can enchant each post with a little extra magick... and no one will be any the wiser!

✦ ✦ ✦

Ease your workload spell jar

A never-ending to-do list can leave you stressed and beyond overwhelmed. This is where we need to make a call to the universe to lighten your load. Make life that little bit easier and your to-do list a whole lot more manageable with this spell to take things off your plate.

What you'll need:

- A corked glass jar
- An incense stick
- A lighter or matches
- Dried lavender (for reducing stress levels and promoting calm vibes)
- Dried mint (for mental clarity and a boost of energy)
- Dried rosemary (for shielding against negativity and harm)
- Dried chamomile (for reducing the feelings of overwhelm)
- Pen and paper
- A white candle (for clarity and cleansing)

What to do:

1. **Cleanse your mind and jar:** It's time to stop stressing over that dreaded to-do list and welcome in a sense of peace and tranquility. The endless tasks are no longer going to be a worry, but will instead feel like a walk in the park. Breathe deeply, and with each exhale allow the sense of stress and dread to leave your mind. Light an incense stick and let the smoke waft around you and the jar to clear any residing negative energies.

2. **Mindfully add your ingredients:** Once you've shifted your mindset around your tasks, take a moment to add each of your herbs into your jar. As you add them (it doesn't matter the order) concentrate solely on the intentions of your ingredients and how each one is going to contribute to easing your workload. Think of how plain sailing life will be now that the pressure is off and that to-do list is getting shorter.

3. **Get intentional:** Next, write the following on your piece of paper:

   'I release the weight of endless tasks. I call in ease, support, and a lightened load. So mote it be.'

   Then fold your paper toward you three times to symbolize bringing your intentions closer to you. With each fold, turn the piece of paper 45 degrees clockwise. This clockwise

motion is great when you're trying to bring something into your life. Pop the piece of paper in your jar.

4. **Seal in the power:** Put the cork lid on your jar, light your white candle, and drip melted wax over the lid, sealing in your spell.

5. **Charge it:** Now that your jar is complete, spend a few minutes getting crystal clear on your intentions and say the following affirmation (you can meditate while doing so) to charge it:

   'My workload lightens as I align with ease, clarity, and flow. I release the pressure to do it all. I trust what truly matters will get done.'

6. **Place with purpose:** Place your spell jar on your desk as a constant reminder that your workload will ease and the sense of dread is no longer needed. Not only will this spell jar help reduce your workload, it will act as a reminder that you don't need to stress – everything will be okay.

MANIFEST A LIFE OF ABUNDANCE

Whether you're calling in a pay rise at work, wanting to land a better job, or hoping that vintage jacket sells for top dollar, you've come to the right place! This section focuses on spells to attract prosperity in all its forms. You'll find spells for good luck, financial freedom, manifesting your dream house, and even conjuring up some quick cash when you need it most – what's not to love above using your witchiness to manifest money?

Quick cash candle spell

Looking to make a quick buck? I'm going to teach you *the* quickest way to manifest money with literally two ingredients, which I'm pretty sure you'll already have in your kitchen right now.

What you'll need:

- 1 tea light
- Ground cinnamon (to attract money and financial prosperity)
- A lighter or matches

I told you it was simple!

What to do:

1. **Visualize money:** Before starting, set your intentions so that they're crystal clear. Really focus on the amount of money you want to manifest, along with the time frame in which you want to receive it. Hold the unlit tea light in your hands and focus on your financial goal. Visualize the money flowing to you effortlessly and quickly.

2. **Get intentional:** Sprinkle a small amount of cinnamon onto the top of the tea light while visualizing your bank account getting fatter. As you're doing so, you can say out loud or in your head the following affirmation:

   'As this candle burns, light up the path to financial abundance. All my doors are open to financial success; nothing stands in my way.'

3. **Light it up:** As you light the tea light, repeat the affirmation or create your own money-attracting mantra. Focus on your exact monetary goal and know with confidence that it's already on its way to you; it's only a matter of time.

4. **Let it burn:** Allow the candle to burn completely while you continue to visualize abundance. If needed, snuff it out and relight it later.

5. **Let it go:** Once the candle has burnt out, dispose of the remnants outside or in a natural space, thanking the universe for the wealth on its way to you.

Witch Tip

Repeat this spell as often as you like until your chosen financial goals arrive in your bank account.

✦ ✦ ✦

Money bowl

Money, money, money… Let's make you a rich witch by welcoming wealth and abundance into your home. A money bowl is a *must have* in any witchy household! So, grab your rice and get ready for prosperity, because it's coming your way.

What you'll need:

- A small bowl
- Moon water (*see recipe on page 228*) or an incense stick
- A lighter or matches
- Uncooked rice (a money-drawing magnet)
- Green food coloring (optional)
- Cinnamon sticks (for fast success and prosperity)
- A bay leaf (for prosperity)
- Pen or marker
- Dried basil (for good luck and financial success)
- Cloves (for good luck and prosperity)

- Cash or coins in your local currencies
- A pyrite crystal (for increasing net worth and positive energies)
- A tea light

What to do:

1. **Set the mood:** Before assembling your money bowl, give it a quick cleanse with either incense or moon water. Take a moment to focus on your financial goals. Hold the bowl in your hands and visualize abundance flowing into your life.

2. **Create the base:** Pour a generous amount of uncooked rice into the bowl, covering the bottom completely. This acts as the foundation, drawing in money and stability. To add a little pizazz to your bowl you can mix your uncooked rice with green food coloring to give it even more of a wealthy vibe!

3. **Add cinnamon sticks:** Place the cinnamon sticks in your bowl, around the edge of the rice, to create a circular shape that symbolizes infinite abundance and financial success.

4. **Get intentional:** Write your specific money intention (e.g. 'Financial freedom' or '$10,000') on the bay leaf with a pen or marker, then gently place it inside the bowl. This

will act as a starting goal for your bowl. Don't feel guilty for writing a bigger sum – you deserve it all!

5. **Sprinkle basil and cloves:** Scatter the dried basil and cloves over the other ingredients, calling in luck, prosperity, and financial stability.

6. **Add money and pyrite:** Place your chosen cash or coins around the inside edge of your bowl, adding to the infinite circle of abundance that you're going to attract. Then pop the pyrite crystal in the center of the bowl, allowing it to radiate wealth-attracting energy (crystals such as malachite and tiger's eye would also work well here).

7. **Activate the bowl:** Hold your hands over the bowl and speak an affirmation, such as:

   'Money flows to me easily and abundantly. I don't work for money; money works for me. My net worth is millions. Every time I want money, it comes to me threefold'.

8. **Boost it:** Place a tea light in the center of your bowl, next to the pyrite crystal, and light it. Use the fiery energy from the candle to boost your money magnetism even further.

9. **Decide where to keep your bowl:** Put your money bowl in a clean and visible space where you'll see it on a daily basis. My recommendation would be right next to the front

entrance of your home on a table or in the back left corner of your house (in feng shui, this is your money corner).

10. **Maintain the energy:** Refresh the bowl on a regular basis by adding in new coins or by stirring the ingredients to activate the energy.

Witch Tip

If you're looking to get more money from your job or your own small business, add a business card too.

✦ ✦ ✦

Pay rise candle spell

Right, let's make sure you get that pay rise. After all, you're working around the clock, doing the best you can at your current job, so who's to say you don't deserve one? We both know that you do!

What you'll need:

+ A green candle (for opportunity and movement)
+ Oil (any cooking oil will do)
+ Ground cinnamon (for prosperity and abundance)
+ Dried basil (for momentum and driving energy forward)
+ Coffee granules (to boost your salary)
+ A bay leaf (for prosperity)
+ A pen
+ A piece of string or twine
+ A plate
+ A lighter or matches

What to do:

1. **Visualize your bag:** Find a place where you won't be interrupted. This is your time to focus on removing anything that's preventing you from getting a pay rise. I want you to spend a few moments visualizing exactly how you're going to feel when you get a boost in income. Make sure your vision is crystal clear. The clearer your vision, the quicker your pay rise will turn up.

2. **Dress your candle:** Start by grabbing your green candle and herbs. I want you to cover that candle in a good layer of each of your ingredients. To help them stick a little better to the candle, add a tiny bit of oil before you sprinkle on your herbs. This will give your candle the magick needed to open those new doors.

3. **Get intentional:** Next, put your candle to the side and take a moment to sit down and really think about what you want to manifest. How much of a pay rise do you want to receive? A sensible and plausible number is best. Get specific and visualize your life as though you already have your higher paycheck. How do you feel? What opportunities open up for you? What choices can you make? Write a number on your bay leaf.

4. **Wrap it:** Using your piece of string or twine, carefully wrap your bay leaf around the candle, making sure it's secured

tightly. This is where all the magick components come together to create one big financial energy source.

5. **Light it up:** Melt the base of your candle (just hold it over a lighter for a few seconds) to stick it to your plate. You can also say the following while lighting your candle:

   'I am valued, my work is recognized, and my financial worth increases effortlessly. Opportunities for a pay rise flow to me with ease. I am deserving of abundance, and my income reflects my skills, dedication, and efforts. As this candle burns, my financial growth is set in motion. Money flows to me rapidly and effortlessly.'

6. **Let it burn:** As the candle burns, spend a moment thinking about your pay rise and how excited it makes you feel to know that your efforts are being recognized and rewarded. Once the candle has burnt fully, blow any remains to the wind, making sure you're focusing on your intentions the entire time.

7. **Sit back and relax:** Your money is on its way!

Banish debts candle spell

It's time to say goodbye to debts, loans, and high interest rates that are currently causing you stress and headaches. This spell is designed to lift the heavy burden of financial strain from your shoulders, so you can breathe easier and move forward without constant worry or looming pressure.

What you'll need:

- A black candle (for protection and banishing)
- Oil (any cooking oil will do)
- Chili powder (for removing unwanted payments)
- Dried lavender (for peace of mind)
- Cloves (for a boost of prosperity and financial stability)
- Salt (to prevent and block any future monetary issues)
- A plate
- A lighter or matches

What to do:

1. **Visualize your debts disappearing:** Find a place where you won't be interrupted. This is your time to focus on removing those pesky debts. Take a moment to really visualize how peaceful and stress-free life will be now that these debts are no longer looming over your head.

2. **Dress your candle:** Start by grabbing your black candle and herbs and spices. I want you to cover that candle in a good layer of each of your ingredients, while constantly focusing on your disappearing debts. To help the herbs and spices stick a little better to the candle, add a tiny bit of oil before you sprinkle them on. This will give your candle the magick needed to make those unwanted payments disappear.

3. **Light it up:** Grasping hold of that debt-disappearing candle, melt the base (just hold it over a lighter for a few seconds) and stick it to your plate. To help those bills vanish faster, you can say the following while lighting your candle:

   'Debt no longer has any power over me. I release all financial burdens and make way for abundance and stability. I don't work for money; money works for me. It flows freely in my direction, and I am in control. Prosperity replaces lack, and I step into a future of wealth, freedom, and security. So it is, and so it shall be.'

4. **Let it burn:** As the candle burns, spend a moment thinking about how stress-free your life is going to be now that there are no hefty payments looming overhead. Once the candle has burnt fully, blow any remains to the wind, making sure you're focusing on your intentions the entire time.

5. **Sit back and relax:** Your new stress-free, financially stable life awaits!

Financial freedom spell

Your road to financial freedom is just around the corner. Imagine all the possibilities and amazing things that you can do now that you have a bottomless pit of money. Sounds perfect, right? Let's get you one step closer to that cash!

What you'll need:

- Pen and paper
- Honey (to attract that bag and make sure it sticks)
- Ground cinnamon (for abundance and wealth)
- Coffee granules (to fast-track financial freedom)
- A fireproof dish
- A lighter or matches
- Tongs (optional)

What to do:

1. **Set the mood:** Find a place where you won't be interrupted. This is your time to focus on removing any negative

thoughts around whether you deserve financial freedom. Replace those negative thoughts – tell yourself you are worthy and deserve it as much as the next person – and start visualizing what your life is going to look like when you have that bottomless pot of cash. How will you spend it? How is it going to impact and change your life?

2. **Embody Picasso:** Grab your paper and pen and draw a road. It doesn't have to be a masterpiece; it can simply be two lines with dashes down the center. However, if you want to make it all artistic, I'm not stopping you. Go for it – add trees, a bench, the entire lot! On the top section of the road, I want you to write 'financial freedom,' and on the bottom section, write your name. Then draw an arrow pointing from your name to 'financial freedom.' This is going to be the symbolism that propels you to prosperity.

3. **Squeeze and sprinkle:** Get your honey and squeeze a little along your road. You can use your fingers to spread the honey further, but each time make sure you're moving up from your name toward the words 'financial freedom.' Next, I want you to take a pinch of your cinnamon and sprinkle it on, then do the same with the coffee granules.

4. **Let it burn:** Hold the paper over your fireproof dish and carefully light the edge of your road with a match or lighter. Allow the piece of paper to burn fully. Please watch your

fingers or use a pair of tongs just in case. Picture your road to financial freedom set directly ahead of you. Say the following words:

'I am on the path to financial freedom. Every step I take leads me to abundance, stability, and success. I release past struggles and welcome new opportunities. Money flows to me effortlessly, and I make wise financial choices. My future is secure, prosperous, and full of endless possibilities. I am financially free.'

5. **Let it go:** Once the paper has burnt fully, blow any remains to the wind, making sure you're focusing on your intentions the entire time.

Witch Tip

Repeat this spell as many times as you need, making sure that each time you draw the road, it gets shorter and shorter in length. This will represent you getting closer and closer to your financial freedom goals.

✦ ✦ ✦

Get paid what you're owed candle spell

I know how frustrating it can be when you've lent someone money out of the goodness of your heart and then trying to get them to pay you back is like getting blood out of a stone. It makes you wish that you'd never done them a favor in the first place… However, stress not, I'm here to help.

What you'll need:

- A gold and a pink candle (two candles, for repayment and reconciliation)
- Ground cinnamon (to speed up the process)
- Oil (any cooking oil will do)
- Cloves (to encourage fairness and financial return)
- A piece of string
- A plate
- Pen and paper
- Tongs (optional)

What to do:

1. **Visualize what you're owed:** Find a place where you won't be interrupted. This is your time to focus amicably on receiving what you're owed. Visualize it coming from a place of peace without having to pester for it.

2. **Dress your candles:** Start by grabbing your candles and herbs. I want you to cover both candles in a good layer of cinnamon, while constantly focusing on what you're owed. Use a little oil to help it stick. You can either grind up the cloves and sprinkle them over the candle, or you can stick them into the sides of each candle.

3. **Light it up:** Use your piece of string to tie the candles together – this helps to bind the two intentions: money and reconciliation. Next, melt the bases of your candles (just hold them over a lighter for a few seconds) and stick them to your plate. Then set the candles alight.

4. **Let it burn:** As the candles burn, write down on a piece of paper the name of the person that owes you money plus the sum that's owed. Gently hover the paper over the flame until it sets alight. Use tongs if you're worried about burning your fingers. Carefully place the burning piece of paper down next to the candle. Spend a moment thinking about how stress-free your life is going to be now that you've been paid what you're owed.

5. **A message to the universe:** Once the candle has burnt fully, blow any remains to the wind, making sure you're focusing on your intentions the entire time. As you blow the ashes away, you can say the following:

   'By the power of fairness and balance, what is owed returns to me. The flow of money is restored.'

And just like that, the spell is done. Now we wait!

Dream house spell jar

I know you've got your eyes on a dream house, so why don't I help you get closer to owning it? This spell doesn't even take that long to do, so let's crack on and start calling in the keys to your future home.

What you'll need:

- A corked glass jar
- Moon water (*see recipe on page 228*)
- Ground cinnamon (to speed up the manifestation)
- An old key
- A photo of your dream home
- A white or green candle (white for new beginnings, green for prosperity)
- A lighter or matches

What to do:

1. **Cleanse the jar:** Let's remove all the dust and residing energies in that glass jar to ensure it's squeaky clean and ready to get you your dream house. Simply wash it out using your ready-made moon water, dry it off, and you're ready to go!

2. **Mindfully add your ingredients:** Once your jar is clean, place both the cinnamon and the key in the jar. When you add the cinnamon, concentrate on bringing in fast success and prosperity.

3. **Add your picture:** Fold the photo of your dream house toward you three times. With each fold, turn the photo 45 degrees clockwise. This clockwise motion is great when you're trying to bring something into your life. Then place it inside your jar. This is going to bring your dream home even closer.

4. **Seal in the power:** After filling your spell jar, pop the cork lid on. Now light your candle and drip melted wax over your lid, sealing your spell. You can repeat affirmations such as:

   'My perfect home is already mine. The universe aligns all things to bring it to me with ease. I am ready to receive, and the doors to my dream home open effortlessly. Abundance flows, and I step into the home meant for me.'

5. **Place with purpose:** Place your spell jar in an area where you're confident it will bring you the most luck. This could be the front entrance to your home, your desk, underneath your pillow… Just go with your gut instinct.

Witch Tip

You can shake your spell jar occasionally to activate its energy or simply meditate with it whenever you have the chance. This will ensure you continue getting closer to your dream house.

✦ ✦ ✦

Manifest a successful business spell jar

Looking to start your own business? Or currently have your own business and want to push it to the next level? Tired of the mundane 9-to-5 and want to start working for yourself? Look no further – I've designed this spell jar to ensure your business is nothing but a complete success.

What you'll need:

- A corked glass jar
- An incense stick
- A lighter or matches
- Coffee granules (to keep you laser focused and energized)
- Ground cinnamon (to build confidence)
- Dried basil (for good luck and success)
- Dried chamomile (for financial abundance and to soothe business stress)

- Dried mint (for prosperity and clarity in decision-making)
- A bay leaf or piece of paper
- A pen
- A green candle (for prosperity)

What to do:

1. **Cleanse your mind and jar:** Let's remove all the worries and self-doubt that come with starting a new business. It's time to shift your mindset to that of a successful and wealthy business owner. Grab an incense stick, light it, and swirl it around yourself and your glass jar. Take a moment to relax your mind and focus on building your empire.

2. **Mindfully add your ingredients:** Once your stress levels settle, take a moment to add the coffee and herbs into your jar. As you add them (it doesn't matter the order) concentrate solely on growing a million-dollar business. Think about how excited and proud you're going to feel when you get your first of many paychecks.

3. **Get intentional:** Once you've added all your ingredients, write on your bay leaf or piece of paper exactly what your business is going to look like, plus the goals you have for it. Be extremely specific. For example:

'I have a million-dollar business that takes 1,000 orders a month.'

If using paper, fold it toward you three times to signal drawing success closer to you. With each fold, turn the piece of paper 45 degrees clockwise. This clockwise motion is great when you're trying to bring something into your life. Then place this note inside your jar. If using a bay leaf, just place it straight inside the jar.

4. **Seal in the power:** After filling your spell jar, pop the cork lid on. Light your candle and drip the melted wax over your lid, sealing your spell.

5. **Charge it:** Now that your jar is complete, spend a few minutes getting crystal clear on your intentions and say the following affirmations:

   'Wealth and opportunity flow to me effortlessly. My business thrives, grows, and prospers every day. I attract loyal customers, abundant sales, and limitless success. I am aligned with prosperity, and financial abundance is mine. So it is, and so it shall be!'

6. **Place with purpose:** Use this spell jar as a constant reminder while you're building your empire that it's going to be a success. Believe in that and yourself, and without a doubt you'll grow your business.

Witch Tip

Carry this spell jar with you whenever you're doing something relating to your business. Place it on your desk, take it with you to meetings… keep it on you as much as you can.

✦ ✦ ✦

Manifest that special item spell jar

Dying to get your hands on one specific item? A Birken bag, a particular watch, or maybe a crystal that you've had your eye on… This spell is your ticket to receiving that item. There are always a couple of materialistic things we have on our wish list, so let's get to work on making it happen.

What you'll need:

+ A corked glass jar
+ Moon water (*see recipe on page 228*) or an incense stick
+ Dried basil (the money magnet)
+ Cinnamon stick (for abundance and good luck)
+ Salt (for cleansing anything that may prevent you from getting what you want)
+ A bay leaf (for prosperity)
+ A photo of what you want to get your hands on

- A green candle (for good luck)
- A lighter or matches

What to do:

1. **Cleanse the jar:** Let's remove all the dust and residing energies in that glass jar to ensure it's squeaky clean and ready to make your wish list a reality. Simply wash it out using your ready-made moon water (or cleanse using an incense stick), dry it off, and you're ready to go.

2. **Mindfully add your ingredients:** Once your jar is clean, take a moment to layer in your herbs and salt. As you add them (it doesn't matter the order) concentrate on each ingredient's properties. For example, when you're adding cinnamon to the jar, focus on bringing in the abundance and luck needed to help you get what you want. With each ingredient added, you're getting closer to your dream item!

3. **Add your picture:** Once all your ingredients have been added, fold your picture toward you three times to symbolize drawing your coveted item closer to you. With each fold, turn the photo 45 degrees clockwise. This clockwise motion is great when you're trying to bring something into your life. Then place the photo inside your jar.

4. **Seal in the power:** After filling your spell jar, pop the cork lid on. Now light your candle and drip the melted wax over the lid, sealing your spell. You can repeat affirmations such as:

   *'The universe aligns all things needed to bring *my special item* into existence. I am ready to receive, and the doors to *my special item* open effortlessly. Abundance flows, and I step into the ownership of whatever I want.'*

5. **Place with purpose:** Place your spell jar in an area where you're confident it will bring you the most amount of luck. This could be the front entrance to your home, your desk, underneath your pillow… Just go with your gut instinct.

Witch Tip

You can shake your spell jar occasionally to activate its energy or simply meditate with it whenever you have the chance. This will ensure you continue getting closer to your dream item.

✦ ✦ ✦

Trip of a lifetime abundance bowl

Fiji, a safari in Africa, or a trek up Mount Everest? Ever wanted to go somewhere specific but everything just seems to get in the way? Well, this manifestation bowl will have you grabbing your passport and packing your suitcase before you know it. So, get your thinking cap on and visualize what your trip of a lifetime will look like, then get ready to go!

What you'll need:

- A small bowl
- Moon water (*see recipe on page 228*) or an incense stick
- A lighter or matches
- Uncooked rice (a money-drawing magnet)
- Green food coloring (optional)
- Cinnamon sticks (for fast success and prosperity)
- A bay leaf (for prosperity)

- Pen or marker
- A picture of the place you want to visit or a map of the location
- Dried basil (for luck and financial success)
- Cash or coins in the appropriate currencies
- A pyrite crystal (for increasing net worth and positive energies)
- A tea light

What to do:

1. **Visualize your trip:** Before assembling your money bowl, give it a quick cleanse with either incense or moon water. Then take a moment to focus on what your trip will look like. Where is it? What would you do? Visualize this in as much detail as possible. Hold the bowl in your hands and imagine abundance flowing into your life.

2. **Create the base:** Pour a generous amount of uncooked rice in the bowl, covering the bottom completely. This acts as the foundation for turning your dream trip into a reality. To add a little pizazz to your bowl, you can mix your uncooked rice with green food coloring to give it a worldly vibe. As

you're doing so, visualize yourself packing your suitcase ready for your dream trip. It's time to get excited!

3. **Add cinnamon sticks:** Place the cinnamon sticks in your bowl, around the edge of the rice to create a circular shape that symbolizes infinite abundance to fund your trip.

4. **Get intentional:** Write your specific trip intention (e.g. 'Fiji for two weeks next year') on the bay leaf with a pen or marker, then gently place it inside the bowl. This will give your bowl direction and purpose. Don't feel guilty for writing a crazy vacation down, you deserve it all! Now add in the picture or map of your destination.

5. **Sprinkle basil:** Scatter the dried basil over the other ingredients, calling in luck, prosperity, and your trip of a lifetime.

6. **Add money and pyrite:** Place your chosen cash or coins around the inside edge of your bowl, adding to the infinite circle of abundance that you're going to attract. Then pop the pyrite crystal on top, allowing it to radiate that Christopher Columbus explorer energy. Crystals such as malachite and tiger's eye would also work well.

7. **Activate the bowl:** Hold your hands over the bowl and say an affirmation, such as:

'I am ready to explore the world and receive the adventure of a lifetime.'

8. **Boost it:** Place a tea light in the center of your bowl, light it, and use the fiery energy from the candle flame to boost your intentions even further.

9. **Decide where to keep your bowl:** Place your manifestation bowl in a clean and visible space where you'll see it on a daily basis. My recommendation would be right next to the front entrance of your home on a table or in the back left corner of your house (in feng shui, this is your money corner).

10. **Maintain the energy:** Refresh the bowl on a regular basis by adding in new coins or by stirring the ingredients to activate the energy.

MANIFEST YOUR INNER MAGICK

Sometimes life can deal a blow that makes you feel powerless and at the mercy of others around you. You may feel like your light has dimmed and your sense of self is slipping away, but the reality is that you are powerful, resilient, and strong. You're in control of your own life. The spells in this section will provide you with a pathway to call back your power and step into your strength – from rituals to restore energy to spells that will sharpen your intuition and allow you to step with confidence into your higher power. You'll also find harmonizing spells that will help you to heal and reconnect with both your feminine and masculine side. This is where you remember what you've always known: The magick is within you.

Confidence booster candle spell

If you've picked this spell, I've got a feeling that your self-esteem has taken a hit recently and you're not feeling your best. Well fear not, I'm going to help you banish this negativity and get your confidence skyrocketing again. There's no reason not to feel confident when you're this badass witch!

What you'll need:

- A red candle (for confidence)
- Oil (any cooking oil will do) or honey (to make sure that confidence sticks)
- Dried chili (for a fiery attitude)
- Rose petals (for self-love and radiancy)
- Salt (to banish low self-esteem)
- A plate
- A lighter or matches

What to do:

1. **Visualize your bad bitch energy:** Find a place where you won't be interrupted. This is your time to focus on getting your spark and fiery energy back. Visualize yourself as the most confident version of you. How would you speak, act, and carry yourself? It's time to start feeling unstoppable.

2. **Dress your candle:** I want you to cover the candle in a good layer of chili, rose petals, and salt. You can use a little olive oil or honey to help your ingredients stick. These are the key ingredients that will give you that bad bitch energy. While you're dressing your candle, think about confidence. Really embody that feeling – let it take over!

3. **Get intentional:** Once you've generously covered your candle, take your lighter, melt the base of the candle slightly, and stick it to your plate. If you have any leftover chili, rose petals, or salt you can sprinkle them around the base of the candle for an extra boost. Before you light your candle, focus on the following affirmations:

   'I am strong, capable, and unstoppable. I trust myself and my abilities. I radiate confidence, and I move through life with power and grace. I believe in myself, and others also see my unstoppable strength. I am untouchable.'

4. **Light it up:** While visualizing your confidence skyrocketing, get a hold of the lighter and set the wick ablaze. Allow the candle to burn fully. It's time to step into your true self and stop worrying about what everyone else thinks. From me to you, you've got this!

Witch Tip

After the candle has finished burning, put any remnants into a little organza bag or spell jar and carry that energy around with you. It will act as a reminder and a guide to keep your confidence levels high.

✦ ✦ ✦

Happiness and positivity candle spell

I hear you're feeling a little down? Don't worry, this spell will help boost your dopamine levels and get you back on track to being your happiest self. I don't like seeing you sad, so let's shift your mindset and bring your spark back!

What you'll need:

- A fresh orange (for happiness and joy)
- A yellow candle (for uplifting energies)
- Oil (any cooking oil will do)
- Salt (to remove negativity)
- Dried chamomile (for self-love and radiancy)
- Dried rosemary (to provide clarity and protection)
- A lighter or matches

What to do:

1. **Say goodbye to sadness:** Find a place where you won't be interrupted. This is your time to focus on getting your spark and happiness back. We're throwing out negativity and low vibrational energies. Allow yourself a moment to clear your head and release anything that's preventing you from being your happiest self.

2. **Dress your candle:** Start by grabbing your orange and candle. Slice off the top half of your orange to create a flat surface. Now, cut a small cross-slit into the exposed top of the orange and wedge your candle into it, so it stands upright. You're more than welcome to snack on the other half as you'll only need one piece for the spell. Next, sprinkle the salt, chamomile, and rosemary over the orange and candle. It doesn't matter the order, just concentrate on each of their properties as you're adding them. Use a little oil to help them stick. While doing so I want you to indulge in your senses. Allow the smell of the orange to clear away any negativity.

3. **Get intentional**: Once you've generously covered your orange-y candle in your herbs, light it while concentrating on the following affirmation. You can repeat this as many times as you like or tailor it to fit your needs:

'I welcome happiness into my life. I radiate joy, love, and positivity.'

4. **Light it up:** Light your candle while visualizing your new and happiest self. Allow the candle to burn down fully then bury the orange and any remnants in the ground or a flowerpot if you have one available. This act of burying the orange is a way of giving back to the earth and sending your message even further into the universe. It also symbolizes allowing your happiness to grow while remaining grounded.

Inner strength candle spell

We all face times in our lives where we don't feel mentally or physically strong enough to handle the things we're currently going through. This spell will act as a beacon and a source of strength that will help you to sail through even the toughest of times. Use this spell to channel your inner strength and harness the power and resilience needed to overcome any difficult situations with grace and ease.

What you'll need:

- Garlic powder (for endurance and protection)
- Dried rosemary (for love and strength)
- Dried basil (for luck)
- A red candle (for courage and energy)
- Oil (any cooking oil will do)
- A plate
- Pen and paper

- A piece of string or thread
- A lighter or matches

What to do:

1. **Set the mood:** Find a place where you can sit with your feelings undisturbed. This is your moment to focus on clearing your mind of any doubts about having the strength to get through this. It's time to get super serious and sure of yourself, knowing that you have the power to get through any difficult situation.

2. **Dress your candle:** Begin by mixing together your garlic, rosemary, and basil. As you're doing so, start embodying your most powerful self. Next, grab your red candle, place it on a plate, and drizzle over a little bit of oil. Then sprinkle over your herby mixture and roll the candle in it until it's fully covered. As always, focus on your intentions during every step.

3. **Draw a rune:** On your piece of paper write your name and draw the Uruz rune (*see page 239*). This rune carries a strong symbolism for strength, endurance, and resilience. Then tie the piece of paper to your candle using a piece of string or thread.

4. **Light it up:** Melt the base of your candle (just wave a lighter under it for a few seconds) to stick it on top of your plate, then as you're visualizing your new and empowered self, set the wick ablaze and watch the flame work its magick. Focus on your intentions and know that with each flicker, you're drawing in strength to help you get through any situation.

5. **Let it burn:** As the candle burns, spend a moment thinking about your intentions, and say the following:

   'I am strong, unshakable, and resilient. No challenge will ever get in my way. I am powerful and I can overcome all obstacles. I can handle literally anything with ease.'

6. **Let it go:** Once you've completed your spell and your candle has burnt fully, it's time to sit back and relax! The hard work has been done; all you have to do now is trust that it will be plain sailing from here on in. You don't need to worry about it anymore.

Call your power back candle spell

It's time to reclaim your personal energy. Whether it has been drained by people, situations, or experiences, now's your chance to self-restore. This spell will help to renew your confidence and bring your inner strength and spirituality back to full power.

What you'll need:

- Salt (for protection and grounding)
- A black or white candle (for protection or purification)
- A plate
- Oil (any cooking oil will do)
- Chili flakes (for that bad bitch energy)
- Coffee granules (for revitalization)
- A small mirror (to reflect your power back to you)
- Pen and paper
- A lighter or matches

What to do:

1. **Set the mood**: Find a place where you can sit with your feelings undisturbed. It's time to rejuvenate and replenish your bad bitch energy.

2. **Dress your candle:** Start by sprinkling the salt in a circle to form a protective barrier around your candle. This will prevent anyone from draining your energy. Next, grab your candle, place it lengthways on a plate, drizzle a little bit of oil over it then sprinkle over the chili and coffee. Roll the candle in any chili and coffee that falls onto the plate until it's fully covered. As always, focus on your intentions during every step.

3. **Light it up:** Place your mirror inside your circle of salt and stick your candle on top of the mirror – melt the base of your candle (wave a lighter under it for a few seconds) to get it to stick. Visualize your most empowered self, set the wick ablaze, and watch the flame work its magick. Focus on your intentions and know that with each flicker, you're bringing your power and strength back to you.

4. **Let it burn:** As your candle burns, spend a moment thinking about your intentions, and say the following:

'I call back my power from all places, people, and situations that have taken from me. My energy is mine, complete

and strong. With this flame, I reclaim all of my strength and power. No one can access my energy but me.'

5. **Let it go:** Once your candle has burnt fully, it's time to sit back and relax. The hard work has been done, and all your power and energy is on its way back to you.

Open your third eye candle spell

This spell is designed to awaken and strengthen your third eye. (But I only have two eyes? Nope, you have three; your third eye, positioned in the middle of your forehead, is your gateway to unstoppable intuition, your higher consciousness and awareness. Pretty cool huh?). It's time to heighten your intuition, deepen your spiritual insights, and enhance your psychic abilities. Let's clear all your blockages, sharpen your perception, and align you with divine wisdom.

What you'll need:

- A purple candle (for spiritual awareness)
- Dried mugwort (to enhance psychic vision)
- Oil (any cooking oil will do)
- Amethyst crystal (to activate the third eye)
- A small mirror (to reflect your inner sight)
- A lighter or matches

What to do:

1. **Visualize your third eye:** Find a place where you won't be interrupted. This is your time to focus on unlocking your third eye and really tapping into your higher consciousness. Set down all your ingredients and open your mind to the idea of unleashing your psychic abilities.

2. **Dress your candle:** Start by grabbing your candle and mugwort. I want you to completely cover that candle in a nice thin layer of mugwort. This will give your purple candle even more of a mystical boost, allowing you to tap into your third eye with greater ease. Use a little oil to help it stick to the candle.

3. **Get intentional:** Next, place your small mirror on a sturdy surface. Then melt the base of your candle ever so slightly (just wave your lighter under it for a few seconds) and stick the candle on top of the mirror. As you're doing so, really visualize your third eye opening and your psychic vision strengthening. You can say the following while doing so:

   'My third eye is open. My intuition is clear. I see beyond the veil with wisdom and trust.'

4. **Light it up:** Place the amethyst on top of the mirror, next to your candle. As you're visualizing your third eye opening, light the wick. Watch the flame work its magick. Focus on

your intentions and know that with each flicker, you're third eye and your intuition are strengthening.

5. **Let it burn:** As your candle burns, spend a moment thinking about your intentions, and say the following:

   'My intuition is strong. My vision is clear. I see beyond the physical, guided by wisdom and truth. My third eye is open, and I trust in my inner knowing.'

   Allow the candle to burn fully, then blow any remains to the wind, making sure you're focusing on your intentions the entire time.

6. **Let it go:** Once you've completed your spell, sit back and relax. You've done the hard work of opening up your third eye, now it's just a matter of time before you can start using it.

Witch Tip

After you've finished your spell, keep your amethyst in your pocket as a powerful reminder that your third eye has been unlocked.

✦ ✦ ✦

Raise your energy candle spell

Are you ready to clear out the old, stagnant energy that's weighing you down and replace it with high vibrational energy? It's time to stop being all doom and gloom and refresh your spirit. This spell is designed to shift you from a low-energy state to a high-vibration and empowered state. Let's get energized!

Ingredients:

- A yellow candle (for happiness and joy)
- Calendula flower (for positivity and high vibrations)
- Coffee granules (for an uplifting mindset)
- Allspice (for self-love, luck, and healing)
- Oil (any cooking oil will do)
- A candle holder
- A lighter or matches

What to do:

1. **Set the mood:** For this spell I want you to bang on your favorite uplifting music playlist and start to get those energy levels rising. Find a place where you won't be interrupted, and where you can dance if you feel the urge to while casting your spell. This is your time to blast away any low vibrations and replace them with positive and uplifting energy. Gather all your ingredients, and let's get to work!

2. **Dress your candle:** I want you to cover that candle in a layer of calendula flower, coffee, and allspice. You can use a little oil to help the herbs stick if needed. These ingredients are going to be key to providing you with an uplifted spirit.

3. **Get intentional:** Hold your herby candle in your hand and really concentrate on charging it with positive and joyful energy. Let go of all the heavy energies that are clearly not good for you. We're saying goodbye to that miserable shit! Say the following affirmation either out loud or in your head:

   'I am vibrant, powerful, and full of light. Energy flows freely through me. I radiate joy, strength, and positivity.'

4. **Light it up:** As you're concentrating on your new and empowered self, place the candle in your candle holder and light the wick. Once lit, you can spend a few minutes

dancing or singing along to your favorite songs as the candle burns. Don't waste your energy feeling silly or awkward; this is your time to listen to your guilty pleasure songs and to really enjoy yourself. The fire from the candle paired with the music is the best way to get those good vibes flowing!

5. **Let it burn:** As your candle burns, spend a moment thinking about your intentions, and say the following:

    'With this flame, I call in high vibrations.
    My energy rises. My spirit glows.'

    Allow the candle to burn fully, then blow any remains to the wind, making sure you're focusing on your intentions the entire time. It's only good vibes from here on in!

Align with your highest self spell jar

It's time to step into your highest self – your most powerful, confident, and intuitive version. This spell jar will help you to clear out any blockages, strengthen your inner wisdom, and align you with your soul's true purpose. Keep it on your altar, bedside, or carry it with you to maintain alignment with your highest path.

What you'll need:

- A corked glass jar
- An incense stick
- A lighter or matches
- Ground cinnamon (for your most abundant self)
- A bay leaf (for manifesting anything you could ever want)
- Dried rosemary (to provide clarity and remove self-doubt)
- Dried chili (for power and confidence)
- Dried lavender (for inner peace and intuition)

- Pen and paper
- A purple candle (to seal in your intentions)

What to do:

1. **Cleanse your mind and jar:** Let's remove all your worries and self-doubt. Grab an incense stick, light it, and swirl it around yourself and your glass jar. Take a moment to relax your mind and focus on tapping into your highest self.

2. **Mindfully add your ingredients:** Once your mindset has shifted to this expansive place, sprinkle each of the herbs into your jar. As you add them (it doesn't matter the order) concentrate solely on the intentions of your ingredients and how they're going to help you reach your highest self. Visualize exactly how your highest self will act and feel, then embody it!

3. **Get intentional:** Once all your ingredients have been added, write down the following on a piece of paper:

   'I fully embrace my highest self. I walk in wisdom, confidence, and clarity. I release doubt and fear. My path is clear.'

   Then fold your paper toward you three times to symbolize bringing your intentions closer to you. With each fold, turn the piece of paper 45 degrees clockwise. This clockwise

motion is great when you're trying to bring something into your life. Add the paper to the jar.

1. **Seal in the power:** After filling your spell jar, pop the cork lid on. Light your candle and drip the melted wax over the lid, sealing in your spell.

5. **Charge it:** Now that your jar is complete, spend a few minutes getting crystal clear on your intentions and say the following affirmations (you can meditate while doing so) to charge your jar:

'As I hold this jar, I also hold the energy of my highest self. I am aligned, powerful, and wise. My path is clear. I am the highest version of myself.'

6. **Place with purpose:** Place your spell jar on your altar, by your bed, or carry it with you. Let it be a constant reminder that you're embodying and envisioning the highest version of yourself.

Shadow work spell jar

It's time to embrace and heal your shadow self – those hidden parts of you, and the deep emotions and past experiences that influence your life. By working alongside your shadow self instead of resisting it, you'll be able to find a deep sense of peace and transform into the best version of yourself. What are you waiting for? Don't be afraid, this is your invitation to heal and grow.

What you'll need:

- A corked glass jar
- An incense stick
- A lighter or matches
- Black salt (for protection) (*see recipe on page 226*)
- Dried mugwort (for insight and accessing subconscious truths)
- Dried rosemary (for clarity and healing old wounds)
- Cloves (for courage to face hidden fears)
- Dried lavender (for grounding and peaceful shadow integration)

- Pen and paper
- A black or dark blue candle (for deep introspection)

What to do:

1. **Cleanse your mind and jar:** Let's remove all your worries and self-doubt, it's time for immense healing and transformation. Grab an incense stick, light it, and swirl it around yourself and your glass jar. Take a moment to relax your mind and focus on tapping into your shadow self. Sit quietly and reflect on the fears, doubts, or wounds you want to acknowledge and heal.

2. **Mindfully add your ingredients:** Once your mindset has shifted to one of acceptance over resistance, take a moment to add the salt and herbs into your jar. As you add them (it doesn't matter the order) concentrate solely on the intentions of your ingredients and how they're going to help you communicate with your shadow self. Think of how you'll feel once you've healed yourself from all past traumas and broken free from the wounds that are holding you back in life.

3. **Add your note:** Next, write the following on a piece of paper:

   'I embrace my shadow with love. I release fear and shame. I integrate my past into my power. I heal, I transform, I grow.'

Then fold your paper toward you three times to symbolize welcoming in your shadow self. With each fold, turn the piece of paper 45 degrees clockwise. Add it to the jar.

4. **Seal in the power:** After filling your spell jar, pop the cork lid on. Light your candle and drip the melted wax over the lid, sealing in your spell.

5. **Charge it**: Now that your jar is complete, spend a few minutes getting crystal clear on your intentions and say the following affirmations (you can meditate while doing so) to charge it:

   'I honor my shadow, for it is a part of me. Through darkness, I find light. Through pain, I find wisdom. I am whole.'

6. **Place with purpose:** Position your spell jar by your bed or somewhere in your personal space. Meditate with it to help you connect with your shadow self and begin to heal.

Witch Tip

This spell jar supports inner healing and transformation, allowing you to release past wounds and step fully into your authentic self. Carry it with you as a reminder to be gentle and patient with yourself.

✦ ✦ ✦

Divine feminine energy candle spell

Tapping into your feminine side will allow you to become more self-aware, get in touch with your creative side, and forge a deeper connection with yourself and the world around you. It will foster emotional intelligence that will lead to a more fulfilling and balanced life. If that sounds appealing, then it's time to well and truly step into your divine feminine energy; to embrace your intuition, creativity, and sensuality. This is the moment to practice self-love and radiate confidence. Reconnect to the part of you that *feels*, *knows*, and *creates* without needing to prove yourself to anyone. Let's feel it out!

What you'll need:

- Pink salt (for protection)
- Pomegranate seeds (the epitome of the divine feminine, embodies Persephone herself)
- A pink candle (for self-love)
- Dried rose petals (for love and emotional healing)

- Dried lavender (for emotional healing and balancing)
- Chili flakes (to embody your most confident and fiery self)
- Oil (any cooking oil will do)
- A candle holder
- A bay leaf (for magick wishes)
- A pen
- A piece of string or thread
- A lighter or matches

What to do:

1. **Set the mood:** For this spell, think soft lighting, your favorite incense burning, and a gentle meditation playlist. Create a safe and tranquil space that will allow you to embrace your softness and relieve lingering stress. This is your time to really get in touch with your feminine side.
2. **Dress your candle:** Start by creating a small circle of salt and pomegranate seeds. This will form a circle of protection around you that also guards your feminine side. Combine the rose petals, lavender, and chili into a little magickal mixture. Then cover your candle in a little bit of oil and sprinkle your herbs on it until it's fully coated. These

ingredients are going to be key to providing you with that divine femininity.

3. **Get intentional:** Take your herby candle and put it in a candle holder in the direct center of the salt circle. Then write the following on your bay leaf:

   'I am the divine feminine.'

   Now tie the bay leaf to your candle. It's time to step into your full feminine era. We're saying goodbye to anything that's holding you back. Say the following affirmation either out loud or in your head:

   'I am the embodiment of grace, wisdom, and power. My intuition is strong, my heart is open, and my energy flows effortlessly. I honor my body, trust my soul, and embrace the magick within me. I am love, I am creation, I am divine.'

4. **Light it up:** As you're concentrating on your intentions, light your candle. Spend a few minutes meditating on the idea of embodying your divine feminine energy. Concentrate on feelings of peace, love, and self-acceptance. Embrace your intuition and trust in yourself. Allow the candle to burn fully, then blow your remaining bits and pieces into the wind. Alternatively, you can sprinkle the ingredients in a nearby stream and allow the current to carry your intentions to the universe.

Divine masculine energy candle spell

Embracing your masculine side is all about becoming your most powerful and strongest self. If it's time to take action and get shit done, this is the spell for you! Problem-solving and making difficult decisions will be so much easier when you tap into your masculine side. Now is not the moment to bury your head in the sand; it's time to step fully into your masculine energy. Drive, determination, and action are the key words here. So, without further ado, let's get this spell done!

What you'll need:

- Black salt (for protection) (*see recipe on page 226*)
- Ground ginger (to fuel your inner fire, confidence, and courage)
- A red candle (for strength, confidence, and clarity)
- Dried rosemary (for mental clarity and direction)
- Dried basil (for success, determination, and abundance)

- Black pepper (to strengthen your determination)
- Oil (any cooking oil will do)
- A candle holder
- A bay leaf (for magick wishes)
- A pen
- A piece of string or thread
- A lighter or matches

What to do:

1. **Set the tone:** For this spell, think soft lighting, your favorite incense burning, and a badass meditation playlist. It's time for business!

2. **Dress your candle:** Start by creating a small circle of salt and ginger. This will form a circle of protection around you that also unlocks your divine masculinity. Next, combine the rosemary, basil, and black pepper into a little magickal mixture. Then cover your candle in a little bit of oil and sprinkle your herbs on top until it's fully coated. These ingredients are going to be key to providing you with that divine masculinity.

3. **Get intentional:** Take your herby candle and put it in a candle holder in the direct center of the salt circle. Then write the following on your bay leaf:

   'I am the divine masculine.'

   Now tie the bay leaf to your candle. It's time to step into your full masculine era. We're saying goodbye to anything that's holding you back. Say the following affirmation either out loud or in your head:

   'I am strong, confident, and fearless. I take bold action with wisdom and purpose. My energy is grounded, my mind is sharp, and my power is unstoppable. I protect, create, and lead with unshakable certainty. I embrace my divine masculine energy and move forward with strength and courage. I am unstoppable.'

4. **Light it up:** As you're concentrating on your intentions, light your candle. Now spend a few minutes meditating on the idea of embodying yourself as an unstoppable force. Concentrate on the feelings of success, determination, and leading with purpose. Embrace your intuition and trust in yourself. Allow the candle to burn fully, then blow your remaining bits and pieces into the wind. Alternatively, you can sprinkle the ingredients in a nearby stream and allow the current to carry your intentions to the universe.

Self-love spell jar

It's time to fall in love with the most important person in your life – you. In this world of endless doom scrolling, comparison, and curated perfection, it's safe to say you might sometimes feel pretty shit about yourself. Maybe you're feeling unworthy, ugly, and just darn miserable. But here's the truth: You are one of a kind. There isn't a single person on this planet that can ever get close to owning your power, beauty, and strength. You are who you're meant to be for a reason, so it's about time I remind you of that and help you fall in love with yourself! Remember, being in love with yourself isn't a bad thing, as some people may say. In fact, it's very healing and comforting when you're perfectly happy with yourself. So, without further ado here's one love spell that you definitely need to cast. And if you've chosen this spell over my 'Get your ex back' spell, I can safely say I'm proud of you!

What you'll need:

- A corked glass jar
- An incense stick
- A lighter or matches

- Pink salt (for energetic protection and gentle grounding)
- Rose petals (to open the heart)
- Dried rosemary (for self-respect and inner strength)
- Dried jasmine (to remind you of your beauty and softness)
- Pen and paper
- A pink candle (for self-love and compassion)

What to do:

1. **Cleanse your mind and jar:** Let's start the process of falling in love with yourself. Grab an incense stick, light it, and swirl it around yourself and your glass jar. Take a moment to relax your mind and focus on tapping into your most calm and tranquil self. Sit quietly and reflect on who you are as a person. Let go of any negative thoughts and feelings you have about yourself.

2. **Mindfully add your ingredients:** Once your mindset has shifted to one of love and acceptance, add the salt, rose petals, and herbs to your jar. As you add them (it doesn't matter the order) concentrate solely on the intentions of your ingredients and how they're going to help you to develop love and affection for yourself. Think of how you'll

feel once you're perfectly comfortable and confident in your own skin. Start embodying it!

3. **Get intentional:** Once all your ingredients have been added, write the following on your piece of paper:

   'My worth is not defined by others – I
   am sacred, powerful, and whole.'

   Then fold your paper toward you three times, to symbolize bringing you closer to self-love. With each fold, turn the piece of paper 45 degrees clockwise. Add it to the jar.

4. **Seal in the power:** After filling your spell jar, pop the cork lid on. Light your candle and drip the melted wax over the lid, sealing in your spell.

5. **Charge it:** Now that your jar is complete, spend a few minutes getting crystal clear on your intentions and say the following affirmation (you can meditate while doing so) to charge it:

   'Love flows through me and around me. I am
   deserving of care, compassion, and joy.'

6. **Place with purpose:** Place your spell jar by your bed. Whenever you feel a little down, let it be a reminder of how important it is to treat yourself with love and compassion.

MANIFEST HEALTHIER RELATIONSHIPS

Whether it's summoning a romantic relationship, improving communication with your partner, or rekindling an old friendship, these spells will help you reach out to the people around you. This section includes spells for love, drawing in soulmates, attracting new friends, reconciling with loved ones, and protecting existing relationships. And, of course, I had to add a little sex magick to help you to spice up the bedroom! I've also included spells to help you let go and move on, because sometimes the universe is giving us a hint, and we should listen.

Find your true love candle spell

Are you at that point in life where you're ready to settle down and find your soulmate? Someone who's just so perfect for you that you can see yourself spending the rest of your life with them? Sometimes it feels like you go on so many dates and meet so many people, but they're just not the one. Well fear not, I'm here to help you find your perfect match. So, get your candle and get ready to meet the love of your life!

What you'll need:

- A fresh apple (for true love)
- A red candle (for love and happiness)
- Salt (to protect your future relationship)
- Dried basil (for romance and a fairy-tale ending)
- Honey (for a sweet and joyful relationship)
- Pen and paper
- A lighter or matches

What to do:

1. **Visualize your ideal partner:** Find a place where you won't be interrupted. This is your time to focus on visualizing your perfect partner. Allow yourself a moment to clear your head and really begin to conjure up a vision of them and what life is going to look like when you're together.

2. **Dress your candle:** Start by grabbing your apple and candle. Cut your apple in half to create a flat base. Now, cut a small cross-slit into the exposed top of the apple and wedge your candle into it, so it stands upright. You're more than welcome to snack on the other half as you'll only need one piece for the spell. Then sprinkle the salt and basil and drizzle the honey over the apple and candle. It doesn't matter the order, just concentrate on each of their properties as you're adding them. While doing so, I want you to indulge in your senses. Allow the smell of the apple and sweet honey to clear away any negativity.

3. **Get intentional:** Now, take your piece of paper and write down every single quality your perfect partner has: What do they look like? What are their personality traits? How would they treat you? Once you've written your list, cut a little hole in the side of your apple half and stuff in the manifestation note.

4. **Light it up:** When you're ready, light your candle while concentrating on your dream partner. Try to picture them as clearly as possible. Feel free to say the following affirmations as you're doing so. You can repeat them as much as you like or tailor them to fit your needs:

   'I am worthy of deep, unconditional love. My heart is open to a partner who aligns with my soul, values, and desires. The universe is guiding us toward each other effortlessly. Love flows to me naturally, and I attract a relationship filled with trust, passion, and harmony. My dream partner is on their way to me now.'

5. **Bury it:** Once your candle has burnt fully, don't throw away your apple just yet! I want you to find a place in your garden or your local park and bury the apple. This acts as an offering to the universe and a way of encouraging your manifestation to grow. If you want, you can add in some of your favorite flowers or seeds – as your seeds grow, so do your intentions of finding your dream partner. Now sit back and wait… they're on their way!

Manifest new friendships spell jar

In this day and age, I feel it's more difficult than ever to make new and meaningful friendships. I designed this spell to say goodbye to surface-level friendships and hello to end-game connections that will last you a lifetime. Creating deep, meaningful relationships with people that are on your energy level is so healing, and having someone who you know will always be in your corner no matter what is such a comforting feeling. One that we're going to manifest today, so grab that spell jar and let's be friends!

What you'll need:

- A corked glass jar
- An incense stick
- A lighter or matches
- Pink salt (for protection)
- Rose petals (for joy and friendships)

+ Dried basil (for trust and loyalty)
+ Cloves (for protection against toxic friendships)
+ Dried lavender (for peaceful and long-lasting connections)
+ Pen and paper
+ A pink candle (for joyful friendships)

What to do:

1. **Cleanse your mind and jar:** Let's remove all your worries around making meaningful friendships. Grab an incense stick, light it, and swirl it around yourself and your glass jar. Take a moment to relax your mind and focus on finding your best friends. Sit quietly and reflect on the kind of people you want to start manifesting into your life.

2. **Mindfully add your ingredients:** Once your mindset has shifted to a welcoming place, take a moment to add the salt, rose petals, and herbs into your jar. As you add each one (it doesn't matter the order) concentrate solely on the intentions of your ingredients and how they're going to help you find those wonderful friendships. Think of how you'll feel once you have them in your life. What kind of people are they? What do you like to do when spending time together? Visualize what life would be like with them in your life, and embody that feeling!

3. **Get intentional:** Write the following on your piece of paper:

   'I attract meaningful, kind, and uplifting friendships that bring joy, trust, and love into my life.'

   Then fold your paper toward you three times to represent bringing your new friendships closer. With each fold, turn the piece of paper 45 degrees clockwise. This clockwise motion is great when you're trying to bring something into your life. Add the affirmation to your jar.

4. **Seal in the power:** After filling your spell jar, pop the lid on. Light your candle and drip the melted wax over the cork lid, sealing in your spell.

5. **Charge it:** Now that your jar is complete, spend a few minutes getting crystal clear on your intentions and say the following affirmations (you can meditate while doing so) to charge it:

   'I welcome meaningful friendships into my life. I attract kind, trustworthy, and supportive people who uplift and inspire me. My circle is filled with love, laughter, and connection. So it is, so it shall be.'

6. **The perfect place:** Place your spell jar by your bed. Use it as a tool to remind you to seek ways to forge new connections.

Witch Tip

If you're looking for friends who have particular hobbies or interests, start going to those places yourself. For example, if you're looking for a friend who will go to yoga with you, start going to yoga by yourself. You're not going to find a yogi pal if you're sat at home in your pajamas!

✦ ✦ ✦

Reconciliation candle spell

It's time to make amends and move forward in your friendships and relationships. There are always ups and downs with our loved ones, and sometimes tensions can get high and relationships can feel strained, which is where this spell comes in handy. It's time to heal those wounds and reconnect with your loved ones. You can use this spell for any relationship in your life – ex lover, friend, family member… you choose.

What you'll need:

- A blue and a pink candle (to represent peace and friendship between you both)
- A marker pen
- A piece of string
- Dried rose petals (for love and emotional healing)
- Pink salt (for protection of the relationship)
- Dried rosemary (for clearing stagnant energy)
- Honey (to sweeten your relationship)

- A plate
- A lighter or matches

What to do:

1. **Set the mood:** This is a time to reconnect and let go of bitterness. Create a safe and tranquil space, a stress-free environment away from arguments and bitterness. Start visualizing your relationship on the mend and how happy both of you will be when you finally reconcile with each other.

2. **Connect your candles:** Start by writing your name on one candle and the name of the person you want to reconcile with on the other candle. Then grab the piece of string and tie both candles together. This symbolizes bringing you closer to one another.

3. **Dress your candles:** Combine the rose petals, salt, and rosemary into a little magickal mixture. Then cover your candle with honey and sprinkle your herbs on top until it's fully coated. These ingredients are going to be key to healing and strengthening your relationship.

4. **Get intentional:** Take your herby candles and slightly melt the bases (just wave a lighter under them for a few seconds) then stick them to your plate. Using any leftover salt, create a salt circle of protection around your candles. While doing so, concentrate on the following affirmations:

'I open my heart to healing and understanding. I release pride, fear, and pain, allowing compassion and connection to flow between us. May peace replace conflict, and love guide us back to one another. What is meant to be will find its way, with clarity, truth, and mutual respect.'

5. **Light it up:** As you're concentrating on your intentions, light your candle. Now spend a few minutes meditating on the idea of healing and mending your relationship. Let go of any animosity and welcome in love and peace. Embrace your intuition and trust in the relationship you had with the other person. Allow the candle to burn fully, then blow your remaining bits and pieces into the wind. Alternatively, you can sprinkle the ingredients in a nearby stream and allow the current to carry your intentions to the universe.

Witch Tip

Over the next few days, watch out for any signs that may help with reconciliation. I once did this spell to reconnect with a friend I had fallen out with. My friend had lost her necklace but a couple of days after doing this spell, I found it. This was the sign I needed to reconnect with her, which in turn helped us reconcile with each other. So, keep your eyes peeled!

✦ ✦ ✦

Get your ex back spell jar

Okay, before I give you the spell to manifest your ex back, take a moment to ponder these questions: Do you really want them back in your life? And were they really that amazing? If your gut instinct says 'no,' maybe go to the self-love spell on page 139 instead. If you answered 'yes,' I grant you permission to keep reading. This spell is designed to encourage your ex back into your life but only if it's meant to be, and if you're *both* low-key wishing to get back together. It's not designed to force someone back against their free will, so think carefully before you cast!

What you'll need:

- A corked glass jar
- An incense stick
- A lighter or matches
- Pen and paper
- Salt (for protection)
- Dried rose petals (for love)

- Dried lavender (for healing and peace)
- Dried rosemary (to cleanse any unwanted negative energy that may still be lingering)
- Chili flakes (to reignite your spark)
- A pink candle (for reconciliation and emotional healing)

What to do:

1. **Cleanse your mind and jar:** Clear any thoughts about how your relationship ended and begin to concentrate on all the good times you had together. Let go of any grudges that you or your ex-partner may hold against each other. Grab an incense stick and swirl it around yourself and your glass jar. Taking a moment to relax your mind and focus on the universe bringing both of you back together.

2. **Get intentional:** Once your vision and intentions are clear, take a moment to write down both of your names on a piece of paper and add it to the spell jar. If you're feeling creative, you can either add a sigil (*see page 232*), rune (*see page 239*), or a love heart to your manifestation note.

3. **Mindfully add your ingredients:** Now add your salt, rose petals, herbs, and chili. As you add each ingredient (it doesn't matter the order) concentrate solely on reconciling with your ex and visualize how life will be once you're back

together. Think about how you've both put the past behind you and now only love and harmony remain.

4. **Seal in the power:** After filling your spell jar, pop the lid on. Light your candle and drip the melted wax over the cork lid, sealing in your spell.

5. **Charge it:** Now that your jar is complete, spend a few minutes getting crystal clear on your intentions and say the following affirmations to charge it:

   'I radiate love, forgiveness, and understanding. If we are meant to be, the universe will guide us back together in perfect timing. I trust that love flows to me effortlessly and that what is mine will always find its way back.'

6. **Place with purpose:** Place your spell jar under your pillow or, even better, carry it with you wherever you go as a constant reminder that what is meant to be will always find its way back to you.

Get noticed candle spell

I'm assuming if you're choosing this spell, you're hoping to get your crush to notice you? I know how you feel – I've been in this position before. There's nothing worse than having a crush on someone and feeling like they don't even know you exist. Well, with this spell, they sure will begin to see you! It's time to break the ice and start moving forward with your crush.

What you'll need:

- A purple candle (for psychic connection)
- A marker pen
- A lighter or matches
- Dried rose petals (for love and emotional connection)
- Ground cinnamon (to spark attraction and a little luck)
- Honey (to sweeten your relationship)
- A plate

What to do:

1. **Visualize getting noticed:** I want you to clear your mind and start imagining your crush taking notice of you. Think about how they're going to notice you – through social media, in person, or some other way. Visualize exactly how it will feel when they finally pay attention to you. Hold on to that feeling and embrace it.

2. **Get intentional:** Start by writing '*Your crush's name* will notice me' onto the candle. As you're doing so, picture their face as clearly as possible as well as them reaching out to you. The clearer your intentions are, the quicker the spell will work!

3. **Dress your candle:** Stick the candle directly on to your plate. To make sure it sticks, you can melt the base of the candle slightly (just wave a lighter under it for a few seconds). Next, grab your rose petals and cinnamon and create a circle around the candle. Then, take your honey and give everything a little drizzle! This will help sweeten the spell and attract your crush toward you.

4. **Light it up:** It's now time to give your spell the power it needs. Light your candle and concentrate on the following affirmations:

'My energy is irresistible, inviting, and magnetic. Let their eyes be drawn to me, their thoughts softened

by desire. May they notice me and feel called to contact me. With harm to none, let this spark grow with ease and simplicity. So mote it be.'

5. **Let it go:** As you candle burns, let go of any doubt that you may have and, with full confidence, welcome the idea of your crush noticing you. Allow the candle to burn fully, then blow your remaining bits and pieces into the wind. By doing so, you're reaffirming to the universe that this is what you want to manifest.

Witch Tip

If you have a photo of your crush, you can tie this to your candle to give your spell an extra boost.

✦ ✦ ✦

Spice up your sex life candle spell

I'm assuming if you're choosing this spell, you're hoping to get a little lucky…? Not only can spicing up your sex life be fun, it's also a great way to boost your confidence and tap into your divine feminine energy. Whether you're already in a relationship and looking to get a little freaky, or you're single and looking to mingle (couldn't help it), then you've come to the right place. There are going to be no dry spells if I'm involved.

What you'll need:

- Pen and paper
- A red candle (for romance and passion)
- A piece of string or thread
- A lighter or matches
- A plate
- Dried rose petals (for sex and sensual attraction)
- Chili flakes (for extra kick and fire)

- Your favorite sensual perfume (ylang-ylang, rose, or jasmine are great)
- Honey (to sweeten that sex life)

What to do:

1. **Set the mood:** For this spell, I want you to tap into your sex goddess alter ego. Embody your most confident, feisty self and harness your divine power. Turn off the main light, light candles around you, and wear something that makes you feel your most confident and sexy. This could be a dress, lingerie, or nothing… you name it. Visualize exactly how you want to spice up your sex life. What does it involve? Who does it include? Get specific.

2. **Get intentional:** Start by writing your name, your partner's name, and what you want to happen on a piece of paper. If you don't have a particular person's name in mind, you could describe what they look like or just not add another name, that's completely fine. As you're doing so, picture how spicy you want your sex life to be… fetishes, new toys, whatever floats your boat. There's zero judgment here. The clearer your intentions are, the quicker the spell will work!

3. **Dress your candle:** Grab your candle and wrap your piece of paper around it, securing it with a piece of string. Then place your candle on a plate, upright. To make sure it sticks

you can melt the base slightly (just wave a lighter under it for a few seconds). Next, I want you to grab both your rose petals and chili and create a circle around the candle. You can do it one at a time or mix them together first and then create your circle. Next, take your honey and give everything a little drizzle! This will help sweeten and spice up your sex life.

4. **Light it up:** It's now time to give your spell the power it needs. Light your candle and concentrate on the following affirmations:

   'I am magnetic, desired, and deeply connected. Passion flows to me and through me with ease. I welcome excitement, intimacy, and pleasure into my life. I am worthy of wild love and soulful connection.'

5. **Get sparks flying:** Once your candle has started burning, grab hold of your perfume and *very carefully* (I mean it) spray the candle three times. It will briefly make the flame bigger and inject your spell with the feistiness your sex life needs.

6. **Let it go:** As you candle burns, concentrate on your intentions. Let go of any doubt that you may have and welcome the idea of a new sex life that's both exciting and fulfilling. Allow the candle to burn fully, then blow your remaining bits and pieces into the wind. By doing

so, you're reaffirming to the universe that this is what you want to manifest.

Witch Tip

If you have a particular person in mind, you can tie a photo of them to your candle to give your spell an extra boost.

✦ ✦ ✦

Protect your relationship spell jar

Sometimes when things are going great, you sit and wonder when everything will go wrong. As though it could be too good to be true. So, to protect your peace of mind and your relationship, I created this spell jar. It's designed to protect your relationship from anything that may negatively affect it, such as third parties, arguments, etc. I've got you covered.

What you'll need:

- A corked glass jar
- An incense stick
- A lighter or matches
- Black salt (for protection)
- Dried rosemary (for fidelity and protection)
- Dried basil (to guard against jealousy and bad intentions)
- Dried lavender (for communication and a peaceful relationship)
- Rose petals (for love and romance)

+ Pen and paper
+ A black candle (for protection and resilience)

What to do:

1. **Cleanse your mind and jar:** Let's banish any negative thoughts you may have about your relationship going wrong. So, grab an incense stick, light it, and swirl it around you and your glass jar. Take a moment to relax your mind. Sit quietly and visualize your relationship in as much detail as you can.

2. **Mindfully add your ingredients:** Once your mindset has shifted to a more positive place, add your salt, herbs, and rose petals to your jar. As you add each one (it doesn't matter the order) concentrate solely on the intentions of your ingredients and how they're going to help you protect your relationship. Think about how you'll feel once all fears that your relationship may go wrong have disappeared. Pretty good, right?

3. **Get intentional:** Write both your name and your partner's name on your piece of paper, along with the following:

   'This jar holds the strength of our bond with each other. May it protect our relationship against all harm, misunderstanding, and negative energy, keeping us enclosed in trust and longevity.'

Then fold your paper toward you three times to represent bringing your intention closer. With each fold, turn the piece of paper 45 degrees clockwise. Add it to your jar.

4. **Seal in the power:** After filling your spell jar, pop the cork lid on. Light your candle and drip the melted wax over the lid, sealing in your spell. As always, concentrate on your intentions.

5. **Charge it:** Now that your jar is complete, spend a few minutes getting crystal clear on your intentions and say the following affirmations (you can meditate while doing so) to charge it:

   'My relationship is strong and unyielding.
   Nothing can get between us.'

6. **Place with purpose:** Place your spell jar under your pillow, so your head sleeps above it at night. It will serve as a protective talisman for your relationship.

Witch Tip

Feel free to ask your partner to create this spell jar with you, as it will help bring peace of mind to them as well. You don't necessarily need them there to create the spell jar, but it'll be extra powerful if they're willing to join in.

✦ ✦ ✦

Let go and move on cord-cutting spell

Sometimes it's difficult to let go of relationships that mean a lot to you; physically, emotionally, and spiritually. I know from personal experience that letting go is unbelievably difficult. Most people say that time heals all wounds, but what if you could do something in the meantime to speed up the process? This is where the cord-cutting spell comes into play, as a way to sever ties energetically between you and another person, situation, or emotion that's no longer serving you. It allows you to remove negative attachments such as anger, sadness, trauma, and obsession. It's time to separate your energies, restore your power, and make space for new beginnings.

What you'll need:

- 2 white candles (to represent each of you)
- A marker pen
- A piece of string
- Salt (for protection)

- A fireproof dish (for your candles)
- A lighter or matches

What to do:

1. **Set the mood:** Create a safe and tranquil space, a stress-free environment where you can ease into the idea of letting go. Take a few deep breaths and make the decision to release all that no longer serves you.

2. **Connect your candles:** Start by writing your name on one candle and the name of the person you want to sever energetic ties with on the other candle. Then grab the piece of string, tie one end of it to one candle, and the other end to the other candle. Leave some space between the two candles to allow the string to dangle. This string represents the connection between you both.

3. **Protect yourself:** Now fill your fireproof dish with salt, then place your candles in the dish. The salt acts as a support for the candles while also providing you with protection as you cast the spell.

4. **Light it up:** When you're ready, light each of your candles while concentrating on the following affirmations:

'I release what no longer serves me. I break free from this connection with peace and strength. Nothing holds me back. I am free from all connections.'

5. **Let it go:** As you're focusing on your intentions and the idea of letting go, allow your candles to continue to burn. As they burn, the flame will get closer and closer to the string. Once it reaches the string, the flame will then begin to burn along it. As the string burns and breaks, so does your connection with this person. Once the string has burnt, allow the candles to also burn down fully to complete the spell, then blow your remaining bits and pieces into the wind.

Cool down tempers candle spell

This spell is perfect for when tensions are high and tempers are short. Whether it's you or your household members feeling agitated, this spell will help neutralize any bad moods and restore the peace.

What you'll need:

- A light blue candle (for tranquility and peace)
- Dried lavender (for soft energy and a stress-free environment)
- Salt (for cleansing negative energy)
- Oil (any cooking oil will do)
- Pen and paper
- A candle holder
- A lighter or matches

What to do:

1. **Set the mood:** Take a moment to remove yourself from the tension and stress and find a place of peace and quiet – even if that means going to the bathroom because people are arguing elsewhere. A place of tranquility away from any chaos will help you to get in the right mindset.

2. **Dress your candle:** Grab your candle and cover it in a good layer of lavender and salt. If you want the herbs to stick a little better to the candle, add a tiny bit of oil before you sprinkle on your herbs. This will give your candle the magic needed to get those tempers extinguished.

3. **Get intentional:** Next, put your candle in a candle holder and take a few moments to really quieten your thoughts and embody peace. Write your name or the name of the person who needs to cool off on the piece of paper and then place it next to your candle.

4. **Light it up:** Now it's time to dispel those tempers. Take a moment to concentrate on your intentions and light your candle. Say the following, either out loud or in your head:

   'I clear all negative energies and call in tranquility
   and peace with this candle. All tempers and
   quarrels have been dissolved. The storm has
   passed, only peace is left. So mote it be!'

5. **Let it go:** Spend a moment focusing on radiating peace and tranquility, letting go of any negative thoughts. Once the candle has burnt fully, blow any remains to the wind.

6. **Sit back and relax:** The arguments and tempers will now begin to subside.

Reinforce your boundaries candle spell

We all know too well that certain people like to cross our boundaries and push the limits. What if I told you there's a spell that would stop people from doing just that? Well, there is! Maintaining and strengthening your boundaries is important, and being able to do so without feeling guilty will allow you to protect your space and stay in your truth. It's time to repel those energy-sucking vampires.

What you'll need:

- Dried rosemary (for energetic shielding)
- Salt (for cleansing negative energy)
- A piece of string (to represent your boundaries)
- A plate
- 4 black candles (for protection and strength)
- A white candle (to represent you)

What to do:

1. **Visualize your boundaries:** Take a moment to start visualizing your boundaries and protecting your space. Think of your boundary as a radiating silver circle that surrounds your entire body. This circle will help repel any energy-sucking vampires trying to cross over into your space. Once you're in the right mindset, it's time to cast your spell.

2. **Set your boundaries:** Start by sprinkling your rosemary and salt on a plate, covering the entire surface. Next, grab hold of your string and place it around the perimeter of your plate (making sure the string stays on the plate). This will act as a visual representation of your boundaries.

3. **Position your candles**: Now grab hold of your black candles and place them inside the circle of string in a square shape, leaving enough room in the middle for your white candle. The black candles act as your energy shield, whereas the white candle represents you. Melting the base of each of your candles will help them to stick to the surface and not fall over (just wave a lighter underneath each one for a few seconds).

4. **Light it up:** Once your candles are ready, it's time to light them all – starting with your white candle, followed by the rest. As the candles burn, say something along the

lines of the following, to help strengthen your boundaries even more:

> *'I am allowed to protect my energy, say "no" without guilt, and put myself first when I need to. My boundaries are respected and not crossed. So mote it be.'*

5. **Let it burn:** As the candles burn, spend a moment concentrating on reinforcing your boundaries against those who are continuously trying to cross them. Your boundaries have now been strengthened. Allow the candles to burn fully.

6. **Sit back and relax:** You'll begin to notice that people will no longer try to push the limit. Your peace is protected and respected.

Strengthen your bond candle spell

Sometimes even the strongest of relationships can drift or veer off balance, leaving you feeling as though the spark between you both has gone… but that's not necessarily the case. It's often still lingering in there somewhere, but life gets in the way, leaving you feeling distant and disconnected. Fear not, I'm here to help! This spell will leave you feeling reconnected and closer than ever to your partner. It will reignite the spark and bring your hearts closer. This spell doesn't have to be for a romantic relationship; it could also apply to friends or even family members.

What you'll need:

- 2 pink (for a friendly/family connection) or 2 red (for a romantic relationship) candles (to represent each of you)
- A marker pen
- Red cord or thread (a symbol of your bond)
- Dried rose petals (for love and emotional healing)
- Pink salt (for protection)

- Dried lavender (for emotional healing)
- Honey (to sweeten your relationship)
- A plate
- A lighter or matches

What to do:

1. **Set the mood:** For this spell, think soft lighting, your favorite incense burning, and a meditation playlist providing a gentle soundtrack. Create a safe and tranquil space, a stress-free environment, perfect for opening up your heart and strengthening the connections with your partner. If you want to, and feel comfortable doing so, you can ask your partner to cast the spell with you.

2. **Connect your candles:** Start by writing your name on one candle and the name of the person you want to reconnect with on the other candle. Then grab the piece of red thread and tie the candles together. This is a visual and spiritual representation of bringing your souls closer together.

3. **Dress your candles:** Combine the rose petals, salt, and lavender into a little magical mixture. Then cover your candles with honey and sprinkle your herbs on top until they're fully coated. These ingredients are going to be key to healing and strengthening your relationship.

4. **Get intentional:** Take your herby candles and stick them upright on a plate. To make sure they stick you can melt the bases slightly (just wave a lighter under them for a few seconds). Create a salt circle of protection around them using any leftover salt. Light your candles and concentrate on the following affirmations:

   'Healing and reconnection flow through this relationship with love, understanding, and passion. As the candles burn together, allow the sparks of our relationship to reignite. Our bond is strong, our connection is deep, and we choose love, patience, and harmony.'

5. **Let it go:** As your candles burn, spend a few minutes meditating on the idea of reconnecting with your partner. Let go of any doubt and distance, and welcome in love and peace. Embrace your intuition and trust in your partner and your relationship. Allow the candle to burn fully, then blow your remaining bits and pieces into the wind. Alternatively, you can sprinkle the ingredients in a nearby stream and allow the current to carry your intentions to the universe.

Heal a broken heart spell jar

If you've turned to this spell, firstly I want to say I'm so sorry you're feeling this way. I know exactly how you're feeling as I've been there myself. Going through a break-up genuinely feels like the world is ending but trust me, you're going to be OK. It'll take time to heal but you're going to come out feeling so much better and stronger. I'm going to teach you how to make a spell jar to help speed up the process and ease the pain. I created this specific recipe for myself when I was going through what felt like hell, and it certainly helped me. So, wipe away your tears, take a deep breath, and gather the ingredients listed below.

What you'll need:

- A corked glass jar
- An incense stick
- A lighter or matches
- Dried rose petals (for love and comfort)
- Dried lavender (to ease your heartache)

- Pink salt (for cleansing and emotional protection)
- A small rose quartz chip or moonstone (for heart healing)
- A bay leaf (for strength and emotional renewal)
- Pen and paper
- A pink candle (for healing and self-love)

What to do:

1. **Cleanse your mind and jar:** It's time to stop dwelling on what has gone and allow yourself to find peace in this moment in time. I know that may feel impossible, but take a few deep breaths, turn on your favorite meditation playlist, and quieten your mind. Once you're grounded in the present moment, cleanse your spell jar and yourself with some incense. Allow the smoke to flow over you and the jar, cleansing you of any negativity and heartache. Concentrate on the smell of the incense.

2. **Mindfully add your ingredients:** Now that you're smelling divine, add the rose petals, herbs, salt, and crystal to your jar. As you add them (it doesn't matter the order) concentrate solely on the intentions of your ingredients and how each one is going to contribute to easing your heartache. Try not to think about the pain you're going through and instead focus on the feelings each ingredient is going to bring.

3. **Get intentional:** Write down the following on a piece of paper:

   'I release this heartbreak and invite peace. I give myself permission to let go and in turn feel love and adoration for myself.'

   Then fold your paper toward you three times to represent drawing your intentions closer. With each fold, turn the piece of paper 45 degrees clockwise. This clockwise motion is great when you're trying to bring something into your life. Add the paper to the jar.

4. **Seal in the power:** After filling your spell jar, pop the lid on. Light your pink candle and drip the melted wax over the lid, sealing in your spell.

5. **Charge it:** Now that your jar is complete, spend a few minutes getting crystal clear on your intentions and say the following affirmations (you can meditate while doing so) to charge your spell jar:

   'I release what no longer serves me. I replace heartache with self-love and tenderness.'

6. **Place with purpose:** Put your spell jar under your pillow and allow it to gradually heal and soften your heart. Healing takes time, but this spell jar makes it that little bit easier. Try

not to focus on the past; instead think of all the exciting and new opportunities that the universe will start to send your way.

Just a little extra note from me… You're bigger and better than them. You're so far out of their league. Please don't worry, the best is yet to come! Take it easy, one day at a time. You're not on your own. The comeback will be better than the setback, I promise.

Lots of love,

Lilly x

MANIFEST PROTECTION AND PEACE

It's time to protect yourself from all things evil and nasty. This chapter will provide you with all the spells that you could ever need to protect yourself and your loved ones (including your pets!) from negative intentions and energies. It also includes spells for protecting your well-being, guarding your energy, and staying safe on your travels. Learn how to banish curses and hexes, bad luck, and negativity in general. It's time to feel shielded, balanced, and at peace.

Self-protection spell jar

Life can be a little unpredictable, so protecting yourself from worst-case scenarios is always a good idea. This self-protection spell jar is designed to protect you from negative situations that may impact your life, whether that's misfortune, negative people, or accidents. Creating a protective talisman to shield you is a great step to take and a must for all witches.

What you'll need:

- An incense stick
- A lighter or matches
- A corked glass jar
- Black salt (for protection) (*see recipe on page 226*)
- Dried rosemary (for shielding against negativity)
- Dried basil (for protection against curses and evil spirits)
- Chili flakes (for protection and to purify spaces)

- Pen and paper
- A black candle (for protection and banishment)

What to do:

1. **Visualize protection:** Set the scene by switching off the big light and turning on your favorite meditation playlist. Grab an incense stick, light it, and swirl it around yourself and your glass jar to cleanse. Once you've created your tranquil space, start visualizing a protective barrier forming around you and your home. It can look however you like – a glowing silver ring, a wall of armor… Whatever your mind goes to, go with that. Visualize and feel it. Your spell jar will generate this barrier.

2. **Mindfully add your ingredients:** Now add the salt, herbs, and spices into your jar. As you add each one (it doesn't matter the order) concentrate solely on the intentions of your ingredients and how each one is going to contribute to your protective wall. Think of how safe and protected you now feel. You are protected against all harm, negativity, and people who have bad intentions.

3. **Get intentional:** Once all your ingredients have been added, write the following on your piece of paper:

'I am divinely protected from all things evil. I am safe and sound; nothing can disrupt my peace and happiness.'

Then fold your paper toward you three times to represent drawing your safety barrier closer. With each fold, turn the piece of paper 45 degrees clockwise. This clockwise motion is great when you're trying to bring something into your life. Add the paper to the jar.

4. **Seal in the power:** After filling your spell jar, pop the cork lid on. Light your black candle and drip the melted wax over the lid, sealing in your spell.

5. **Charge it:** Now that your jar is complete, spend a few minutes getting crystal clear on your intentions and say the following affirmations (you can meditate while doing so) to charge your spell jar:

   'I am safe, I am protected, I am divinely guided. No harm can touch me, no negativity can enter my space. I am surrounded by light, shielded by love, and grounded in strength. Only positive energy is welcome in my life. I am powerful, I am secure, I am unshakable.'

6. **Place with purpose:** Position your spell jar by the entrance of your home to ensure the protective barrier remains intact. If you want, you can create multiple self-protection

spell jars and place each one by the entrances to your home. Or you could keep one on you at all times.

Witch Tip

If you're going to carry the spell jar around with you, you could use a smaller jar and tie it to a necklace.

✦ ✦ ✦

Pet protection spell jar

If you're a pet owner, you know exactly how I feel about this spell jar. Your furry companion is your best friend, your therapist, and quite frankly the love of your life. The idea of something happening to them is honestly soul destroying. I created this spell jar to protect my own furry friends: Ginny (Morkie), Tarot, and Theodore (my witch's cats). I made one for each of them and placed it underneath their beds. Creating a spell jar for your pets helps put your mind at ease, giving you more time to cherish them rather than worrying about their well-being.

What you'll need:

- A corked glass jar
- Moon water (*see recipe on page 228*)
- Pink salt (to ward off harm)
- Dried rosemary (for shielding against harm and fatality)
- Dried basil (for good health and vitality)
- Catnip (acts as a barrier against harm and evil)

- Your pet's fur (only a little bit, let's not scalp them…)
- Pen and paper
- A black candle (for protection and banishment)
- A lighter or matches

What to do:

1. **Cleanse your jar:** Let's remove all the dust and residing energies in that glass jar to ensure it's squeaky clean. Simply wash it out using your ready-made moon water, dry it off, and you're ready to go.

2. **Visualize protection:** Start visualizing a protective barrier forming around your pet. It can look however you like – a glowing silver ring, a wall of armor… Whatever your mind goes to, go with that! Visualize it, really feel it, and your spell jar will generate this barrier. You could always have your furry friend in the room with you to ensure your intentions are crystal clear.

3. **Mindfully add your ingredients:** Now add your salt and each of your herbs into your jar. As you add each one (it doesn't matter the order) concentrate solely on the intentions of your ingredients and how each one is going to contribute to protecting your pet. Think of how safe and

stress-free you're going to feel knowing they're divinely protected against all harm.

4. **Get intentional:** Once all your ingredients have been added, grab a couple of strands of their fur and add it to the jar. Then write the following on your piece of paper:

   *'*Name* is divinely protected. Their health, body, and soul are guarded. So mote it be.'*

   Then fold your paper toward you three times to represent bringing the safety barrier closer. With each fold, turn the piece of paper 45 degrees clockwise. Add it to your jar.

5. **Seal in the power:** After filling your spell jar, pop the cork lid on. Light your black candle and drip the melted wax over the lid, sealing in your spell.

6. **Charge it:** Now that your jar is complete, spend a few minutes getting crystal clear on your intentions and say the following affirmations (you can meditate while doing so) to charge your spell jar:

   *'*Name* is safe, protected, and divinely guarded. No harm will come to them, and zero negative energy can reach them. They are surrounded by love and light, their protective barrier is unshakable. They cannot be touched by anything that may bring them harm. *Name* is protected.'*

7. **Place with purpose:** Position your spell jar underneath you pet's bed or near wherever they usually sleep (under my bed in Ginny's case), or by their water bowl. You can create a spell jar for each of your pets, or you can add them all into one jar. It's entirely up to you; both options will keep your precious bundles safe from harm.

Protect your loved ones candle spell

If you're looking to protect your entire family or all your friends from negativity, this spell is perfect. It will help generate a protective shield around all of them; a shield of love, peace, and safety. Whether you want to prevent unwanted drama or protect your loved ones from all negative things in general, this spell will help give you the peace of mind that they're safe. You can add yourself into this spell, too, if you'd like.

What you'll need:

- Black candles (one for each person you want to protect)
- A marker pen
- A plate
- Dried rose petals (for love and happiness)
- Salt (to provide protection and cleansing of negativity)
- String (to create a barrier of protection)
- A lighter or matches

What to do:

1. **Visualize protection:** Take a moment to set the scene – start picturing each of your loved ones as clearly as possible in your mind. Concentrate on the things you want to shield them against: a specific person, a situation, or illness, for example. Visualize this protective shield reaching them wherever they are in the world.

2. **Get intentional**: Take one black candle for each person you want to protect. Write that person's name on their candle, then draw the Algiz rune (*see page 240*) beneath their name. While you're doing so, picture each person's face as clearly as possible, as well as the protective shield surrounding them. This shield could be a silver glow, a wall of armor, or whatever your mind is drawn to. The clearer your intentions are, the quicker the spell will work!

3. **Create your circle of protection:** Grab each of your candles and stick them directly on a plate to form a circular shape. To make sure they stick, you can melt the bases of the candles slightly (wave a lighter under them for a few seconds). Next, I want you to gather your rose petals, rosemary, and salt and sprinkle them in a circle around the candles. You can do it one at a time or mix them together first and then create your circle. After you've done this, take your string and place it around the outside of the candles, making sure to

knot the two ends together. This is going to symbolize your infinite circle of protection.

4. **Light it up:** It's now time to give your spell the power it needs. Light your candles and while doing so, concentrate on the following affirmation:

   *'I create this circle of protection around *names* to ensure they are divinely protected. They are guarded from harm both seen and unseen. They are all infinitely protected. So mote it be.'*

5. **Let it go:** As your candles burn, concentrate on your intentions. Let go of any doubt that your loved ones may be harmed and know that they're now infinitely protected in mind, body, and soul. Allow the candles to burn fully, then blow your remaining bits and pieces into the wind. By doing so, you're reaffirming to the universe that this is what you want to manifest.

Witch Tip

If you have photos of your loved ones, you can place them in the middle of your circle of candles to give your spell even more direction.

✦ ✦ ✦

Banish hexes and curses fire spell

Within witchcraft, it's important to know how to banish hexes and protect yourself from evil. This spell helps to seal your aura and protect you from unwanted attacks. This could be the evil eye someone has sent you, a curse someone has muttered under their breath… the list of possibilities is endless. So, like the badass witch that you are, let's not give anybody the chance to even *think* about hexing you. With your strength and power, this spell will be a walk in the park.

What you'll need:

- A fireproof dish (a cauldron if you have one)
- Dried chili (to banish hexes and curses)
- Dried rosemary (for clarity and energy clearing)
- Dried sage (for physical protection and aura protection)
- Black peppercorns (to block people with ill intentions)
- Salt (to create a protective barrier)

- Pen and paper
- A lighter or matches

What to do:

1. **Set the mood:** Find a place where you won't be interrupted. This is your time to focus on banishing any hexes or curses that may have entered your life. Take a moment to visualize how peaceful and stress-free life will be now that negative energy is no longer looming over your head.
2. **Mindfully add your ingredients:** Sprinkle all your herbs and spices into the cauldron while focusing on their properties and how they will help to remove hexes and curses from your life.
3. **Get intentional:** Next, get your piece of paper and write down all the things you want to banish from your life. If you know what the hex is, write that down. If you don't, just write:

   'I banish all past, current, and future
   hexes from my life and home.'

   You can write down as much or as little as you like. Once you've written everything down, set your paper on fire, and then throw it into the cauldron with everything else. The dried herbs should also begin to catch fire.

With your smoking cauldron in hand, walk around your home counterclockwise, letting the smoke remove any lingering negative energy. Go around each room counterclockwise, one room at a time. To help those hexes vanish faster, say the following while smoke-cleansing your home:

'All hexes are broken, all curses undone.
No harm can reside within this home. Both my home
and myself are shielded from all things evil.
Only love and happiness is welcome. Allow evil
to retreat and dark energy to fade. My home and
I are fully protected from anything
that may come my way.'

4. **Let it go:** As the herbs and piece of paper burn, spend a moment thinking about how peaceful life will be now, knowing you're divinely protected from harm. Once everything has burnt down, blow the ashes to the wind, making sure you're focusing on your intentions the entire time.

5. **Sit back and relax:** Your new divinely protected life awaits!

Witch Tip

After casting this spell, you can sprinkle salt across the entrances to your home, providing an extra physical barrier against anything that may come your way in the future. You can refresh this salt barrier as often as you like.

✦ ✦ ✦

Protection from the evil eye spell jar

'What is the evil eye?' you may ask. The evil eye is rooted in many cultures and is based on the idea that through this malevolent glare, someone can either intentionally or unintentionally send negative energy or cause harm to another person. This could be wishing ill on their success or happiness, often prompted by envy. It's thought that this negative energy can bring misfortune or bad luck. So, protecting yourself is vital, and this is where this custom spell jar comes in handy, as it will do just that.

What you'll need:

- A corked glass jar
- An incense stick (optional)
- A lighter or matches (if using incense to cleanse)
- Dried mugwort (to create a psychic shield of protection)
- Dried rosemary (to cleanse your space of negative energy)
- Garlic (to protect against ill intentions)

- Fennel (for deflecting the evil eye and curses)
- 3 bay leaves (to act as a barrier against harm and evil)
- A pen
- A black and blue candle (for protection and banishment)

What to do:

1. **Cleanse your mind and jar:** It's time to banish any unwanted negative intentions coming your way, so start off by cleansing yourself and your jar. You can do this by using sound (by clapping or banging on pots and pans to remove static energy) or by burning incense. Give yourself a good cleanse to banish any negativity that may be lingering around you. You could even take a cleansing shower beforehand if you feel it's necessary.

2. **Mindfully add your ingredients:** Once you're squeaky clean, take a moment to add the mugwort, rosemary, garlic and fennel to your jar. As you add each ingredient (it doesn't matter the order) concentrate solely on the intentions of your ingredients and how each one is going to contribute to protecting you against the evil eye.

3. **Get intentional:** Next, grab your bay leaves and draw a simple eye on one, the Algiz rune on another (*see page 240*),

and on the third write your name followed by 'I am protected.' Add the bay leaves to the jar.

4. **Seal in the power:** After filling your spell jar, pop the cork lid on. Light your candles and drip the wax from both candles over the lid, sealing in your spell. As you're doing so, visualize yourself now protected from the evil eye.

5. **Charge it:** Now that your jar is complete, spend a few minutes getting crystal clear on your intentions and channel your energy into it. Focus on protecting yourself from the evil eye.

6. **Place with purpose:** Finally, place your spell jar somewhere within your home, either by the entrance or where you spend most of your time. Alternatively, you can carry it with you from day to day. If you've used a small glass jar, make sure to wrap it in a protective cloth or a little bit of bubble wrap to prevent it from accidentally getting smashed in your bag or pocket.

Return-to-sender candle spell

People don't always have your best intentions at heart and sometimes might treat you in a way that's undeserved. For example, someone might cheat on you, spread lies and rumors, or just simply send you negative energy. A return-to-sender spell is a type of protection and reversal spell that's used to reflect any negative energy back to the original sender: 'What you send to me, returns to thee.' So, let's put a stop to these negative people and keep you safe from harm.

What you'll need:

- A small mirror (to send the energy right back)
- A lemon (for cleansing negative energy)
- A black candle (for protection and banishing)
- Salt (to protect your future self from further negativity)
- Chili flakes (to send a 'sting' back to the original sender)
- 3 nails or drawing pins (to pierce the negative energy)
- A lighter or matches

What to do:

1. **Set the mood:** Find a quiet place where you won't be interrupted. This is your time to focus on sending that negative energy back to its rightful owner. Get crystal clear on what type of negativity they've been sending your way and get ready to send it right back.

2. **Prepare your candle:** Start by grabbing your mirror and lemon. Place the lemon whole on top of the mirror and slice off the top half to create a flat surface. Now, cut a small cross-slit into the exposed top of the lemon and wedge your candle into it, so it stands upright. Placing your spell on top of the mirror will allow you to send the energy of the spell directly to your sender through a mirror in their home. Mirrors act as portals of energy and are the easiest way to send a magickal message.

3. **Get intentional:** Now it's time to add a little spice. Grab your salt and chili and sprinkle it over the lemon and the mirror. While doing so, think of your intentions as clearly as you possibly can. Afterwards, grab your nails or drawing pins and pierce the lemon with each of them. You can arrange them however you'd like.

4. **Light it up:** When you're ready, light your candle while concentrating on sending that energy right back. Try to picture the sender as clearly as possible, how they made you

feel, and how you want to send all that negativity straight back to them. Feel free to say the following affirmations. You can repeat these as much as you like or tailor them to fit your needs:

'I do not accept this energy. What has been sent to me has now been returned to its original sender via this mirror. I am protected against all harm. I am untouchable and divinely protected. Nothing can break through my protective barriers; everything is reflected back.'

5. **Let it go:** Once your candle has burnt fully, discard your entire spell minus the mirror. You can do this by placing it in the trash and making a note to watch the bin collectors take it away. Or you can simply discard it in a place away from your home. If you're discarding it in nature, make sure to remove the nails and place them safely in a trash can to prevent any wildlife being harmed.

Witch Tip

Cast this spell on your waste collection day, or on either a Tuesday or during a waning moon phase. These are great times for banishment and return-to-sender spells (*see my timing correspondence chart on pages 244-46*).

✦ ✦ ✦

Reveal the truth spell jar

Sometimes the truth needs to be revealed. Whether someone is hiding their true colors or they're simply flat-out lying to your face, uncovering the truth of a situation is important for both healing and growth. If your gut is sounding alarm bells and you desperately need to find out the truth, this spell jar is for you!

What you'll need:

- A corked glass jar
- Moon water (*see recipe on page 228*) or incense
- A lighter or matches (if using incense to cleanse)
- Pen and paper
- Dried rosemary (for clarification)
- Dried mugwort (enhances intuition and reveals hidden truths)
- Dried chamomile (calms emotional noise so the truth can emerge clearly)

- Cloves (strengthens communication and brings honesty forward)
- A blue candle (for communication and truth revealing)

What to do:

1. **Cleanse your mind and jar:** Right, let's get this liar to reveal their true colors. As always, make sure you're in a stable emotional state (we don't need tears while casting this spell, we want the truth!). Let's remove all the dust and residing energies in that glass jar to ensure it's squeaky clean and ready to help you unveil the truth. Simply wash it out using your ready-made moon water (or cleanse using an incense stick), dry it off, and you're ready to go. Now get crystal clear on your intentions around the person with the ever-growing nose (Pinocchio reference if you didn't get it).

2. **Put the liar in the jar:** First off, write down that lil' liars name on a piece of paper and add it to the jar. I would withhold writing down what you think they're lying about as this can limit the truth. We want to find out everything they're covering up, not just a little part of it, especially if you're suspicious of your partner cheating on you. Let's be honest, this is what most of us will use this kind of spell for…

3. **Mindfully add your ingredients:** Now gather your herbs and pile them in the jar, on top of the note with the liar's name. Picture the truth revealing itself to you as clearly as possible, whether that's the person coming forward or you finding out another way. Add each ingredient while concentrating on revealing the truth.

4. **Seal in the power:** After filling your spell jar, pop the lid on. Light your candle and drip the melted wax over the cork lid, sealing your spell. You can repeat affirmations such as:

   'I'm ready to see things clearly now. I open myself to the truth, no matter what it is. I release fear, confusion, and illusions. Let what's hidden come into the light. I trust that clarity will come, and I will know what I need to know.'

5. **Place with purpose:** Place your spell jar somewhere you'll see on a regular basis. Make sure it's positioned off the ground and in a visible space. It will then act as a talisman for revealing the truth.

6. **Sit back and relax:** Now that the hard work has been done, you don't need to go poking and prodding for the truth… it will find its way to you.

Witch Tip

You can shake the spell jar occasionally to activate its energy or simply meditate with it whenever you have the chance if you feel like it isn't working to its full potential.

✦ ✦ ✦

Banishing burnout candle spell

I know exactly how you're feeling right now. The number of times I've suffered from burnout is ridiculous. Not only does it put a halt on our productivity levels, it also destroys our creativity. So, let's make sure we banish that sluggish energy and bring back the creative and determined mastermind that you are!

What you'll need:

- A bowl of water
- A lemon (for invigorating and refreshing energies)
- A pinch of salt (to banish negative energy)
- A piece of paper with your name on it
- A tea light
- A lighter or matches

Alternative: Instead of casting this spell in a bowl, you could fill up your bathtub and cleanse your entire body. Follow *italics* for this adaptation.

What to do:

1. **Set the mood:** Take a moment to find a quiet spot where you won't be distracted. Turn on your favorite meditation playlist and take a few deep breaths. Allow any stress to disappear with each exhale.

2. **Soak in salt water:** Sprinkle your salt into the bowl of water, then place the piece of paper with your name on into the bowl. To charge the water with invigorating power and refreshing energies, add a squeeze of lemon juice. The lemony salt water surrounding your name will cleanse you of any burnout that you're currently experiencing, leaving you feeling refreshed and raring to go. (*If you're running a bath instead, you don't need the paper, just get straight in the water.*)

3. **Light it up:** Place the tea light in the bowl on top of your name. Make sure that the water doesn't cover your candle or you won't be able to light it. The candle symbolizes igniting the energy you need to pull yourself out of your burnout phase. Light that candle! (*If you're opting for the bath option, simply place the tea light on the side of your bath rather than in the water.*)

4. **Get intentional:** Once everything is in place, allow yourself time to sit with the candle and focus on replenishing your energy and creativity.

5. **Let it go:** When you're ready, blow out the candle and visualize your stress fading away. Empty the bowl of water down the drain and imagine it washing away any remaining burnout.

Witch Tip

While casting your cleansing spell, place a piece of clear quartz in the water. Carry on with the spell as stated above and once you've finished, keep the clear quartz as a reminder of your renewed energy.

✦ ✦ ✦

Get a good night's sleep spell jar

Sometimes getting a good night's sleep feels impossible. It doesn't matter how many hours you try and rack up, or how great your sleep hygiene is, you're still left tossing and turning, and then inevitably wake up tired and groggy. What if I told you I could help you out? Because I promise you, I can. So, grab your spell jar, and get ready for the best night's sleep of your life!

What you'll need:

+ A corked glass jar
+ Moon water (*see recipe on page 228*) or an incense stick
+ A lighter or matches (if using incense to cleanse)
+ Dried lavender (the ultimate sleep-well herb)
+ Dried chamomile (for relaxation and easing anxiety)
+ Dried mugwort (for the most magickal of dreams)
+ Salt (for energetic cleansing)
+ A purple candle (for peace and tranquility)

What to do:

1. **Cleanse the jar:** Let's remove all the dust and residing energies in that glass jar to ensure it's squeaky clean and ready to help you get the best night's sleep possible. Simply wash it out using your ready-made moon water (or cleanse using an incense stick) dry it off, and you're ready to go!

2. **Mindfully add your ingredients:** Take a moment to relax your mind and get yourself in a tranquil state (there's no point doing this spell when you're over-energized or stressed – we want chilled and relaxed vibes). Layer in your herbs and salt, and as you add them (it doesn't matter the order) concentrate on each ingredient's properties. For example, when you're adding the lavender, focus on clearing your mind and beginning to relax. With each ingredient added, you're getting closer to a peaceful night's sleep.

3. **Seal in the power:** After filling your spell jar, pop the cork lid on. Light your candle and drip the melted wax over the lid, sealing your spell. You can repeat affirmations such as:

   'I invite peaceful rest, deep sleep, and sweet dreams. My body and mind are safe to relax.'

4. **Place with purpose:** I don't want to point out the obvious, but under your pillow is the optimal place for putting your sleepy spell jar. As you sleep, the spell jar's energies will

radiate through your pillow, providing you with the well-deserved rest that you need. Relax your mind knowing that you're going to wake up feeling energized and rejuvenated. Goodnight, sleeping beauty.

Witch Tip

If you know someone who struggles with getting a good night's rest, I'm sure they'd appreciate you gifting them this little spell jar knowing that it will help.

✦ ✦ ✦

Put your mind at ease candle spell

We all have things that play on our mind on a daily basis, and these thoughts always seem to crop up at the worst times. Having too many things on your mind can cause you to become stressed, anxious, and overwhelmed. But what if I told you that I have a spell to help calm your thoughts and put your mind at ease? Well, we both know I do! So, grab the bits and peaces (yes, I'm aware of the spelling) and let's put your restless mind at ease.

What you'll need:

+ Pen and paper
+ A blue candle (for peace and tranquility)
+ Oil (any cooking oil will do)
+ Salt (to cleanse restless energies)
+ Dried lavender (for removing stress and easing worry)
+ A plate

- A lighter or matches
- Tongs (optional)

What to do:

1. **Outline your worries:** First things first, we need to get rid of all those worries and thoughts that have been driving you crazy all day. To do this, I want you to grab your piece of paper and write down everything that has been bothering you today… and yes, I mean *everything*! Your ex living rent-free, an upcoming deadline that you're stressing about, an event on the horizon that you'd rather stick pins in your eyes than go to… This piece of paper is where you're going to dump all of your worries so that they're no longer taking up brain space. Once you've done this, place the list to one side while you prepare your candle.

2. **Dress your candle:** Start by coating your candle in the oil, salt, and lavender. Once it's well covered, melt the base a little (wave a lighter under it for a few seconds) and stick it to your plate. It doesn't matter if it's not perfect and some of the lavender petals are falling off; it's the intention that counts, remember. Sprinkle more salt and lavender around the candle until you feel as though it's radiating peaceful vibes.

3. **Light it up:** When you're ready, light that candle. Then grab the sheet of pesky worries that you wrote down earlier – we're going to burn it until it's just a pile of ashes. Hold it above the candle and allow it to burn while visualizing all your thoughts and worries burning away. Please do so carefully, using tongs if you like (don't burn your fingers, it hurts!). Once the paper has burnt down to ashes, you can either dispose of these immediately in the trash or leave them until the candle has burnt fully.

4. **Welcome in peace:** Now concentrate on quietening your mind and allowing your worries to disappear. They have all been burnt away so there's now space for you to welcome in peace and tranquility. Say out loud or in your head:

   'I release what no longer serves me. My mind is clear, my heart is steady, and I am safe in the energy of stillness and tranquility'

5. **Let it go:** Once your candle has burnt fully, any leftover candle wax and ashes can be discarded in the trash. If you have any leftover lavender, feel free to sprinkle it under your pillow at night to help keep those worries at bay.

Keep safe on the move spell jar

I don't know about you, but when I'm on the move, I like to know I've got a little extra protection riding with me. Whether you're driving, biking, taking the train, flying, or just constantly on the go, this spell jar is designed to keep you safe from bumps, bad vibes, and unexpected detours. Tuck it into your glove compartment, backpack, or luggage – and make a few extras for friends or family who are venturing out and about. A little magick goes a long way to protecting you when you're on the road (or in the air… or on the rails).

What you'll need:

+ A corked glass jar
+ Moon water (*see recipe on page 228*) or incense
+ A lighter or matches (if using incense to cleanse)
+ A green candle (for protection)
+ Dried basil (the ultimate good luck herb)

- A cinnamon stick (for good luck and safety)
- Dried rosemary (for protection against others while traveling)
- Salt (for protection)
- A bay leaf (for protection)
- A black pen

What to do:

1. **Cleanse the jar:** Let's remove all the dust and residing energies in that glass jar to ensure it's squeaky clean and ready to make you the most protected traveler out there. (A little side note, this doesn't mean you can now drive like a maniac; road safety is still needed.) Simply wash out the jar using your ready-made moon water (or cleanse using an incense stick), dry it off, and you're ready to go!

2. **Mindfully add your ingredients:** Once your jar is clean, take a moment to layer in your herbs and salt, but not your bay leaf just yet. As you add them (it doesn't matter the order) concentrate on each ingredient's properties. Like when you're adding cinnamon to the jar, focus on bringing in good luck and safety when traveling.

3. **Get intentional:** Once all your ingredients have been added, draw the Algiz rune (*see page 240*) onto your bay leaf using black ink and then place it inside your jar. This is going to steer your spell in the direction of safety when traveling (pun intended).

4. **Seal in the power:** After filling your spell jar, pop the cork lid on. Now light your candle and drip the melted wax over the lid, sealing your spell. You can repeat affirmations such as:

   'Every journey is safe, and I arrive with ease. Each time I travel I am divinely guided, I am protected, and I am safe.'

5. **Place with purpose:** Put your spell jar somewhere within your car – this could be your glove compartment, or you could stick it to your dash. Or carry it with you in your backpack or put it in your suitcase.

ADDITIONAL RECIPES, TOOLS, AND CHARTS

BLACK SALT

Black salt is a popular tool used within witchcraft to aid protection and banishment spells. It can also be scattered around the perimeter of your home to protect it from negative energies and unwanted visitors. Think of the spiritual properties of normal salt then multiply it by a hundred.

What you'll need:

- Salt (for purification and protection)
- Incense ash or coal (to amplify intent)
- Chili flakes (a curse and hex repellent)
- Dried rosemary (for cleansing negative energy)
- Black pepper (for protection against harm)
- An airtight container

What to do:

1. Simply mix all of the ingredients together and pour into an airtight container, and there you have it: your very own blend of black salt.

Witch Tip

You could also keep your black salt in a bowl that you use as an incense holder. Then, every time you light a stick of incense you're collecting the ash, which combines with the black salt to amplify its energetic intent.

✦ ✦ ✦

MOON WATER

If you thought making black salt was easy, just you wait, moon water is even easier. But first, what is moon water? It's essentially water that has been blessed underneath the moon, often used in witchcraft for cleansing lingering energies on your tools. For example, before creating a spell jar, simply giving the jar a quick clean with moon water will remove any lingering, unwanted energies that could affect your spell jar's efficiency. Think of moon water as a way of sterilizing your witchcraft tools before you use them in a spell.

What you'll need:

- A clean container
- Water
- A sealed jar (or drinking bottle)

What to do:

1. Fill a clean container with water and place it under the moonlight overnight, ideally during a full moon. As you do this, set your intention. Focus on what you'd like the moon water to support: clarity, calm, creativity, protection – whatever you're calling in. You can speak your intention out loud, whisper it into the water, or simply hold it in your mind as you place the jar beneath the moon.

2. In the morning, store it in a sealed jar ready for use in your spellwork. You can also drink moon water. Simply place a bottle of drinking water underneath the moon, with intention. For example, you can charge the water with the intention of abundance, so every time you take a sip from that bottle you're doing so with the intention of becoming more abundant.

Witch Tip

There are many different uses for moon water – cleansing, drinking, and cooking are just a few. You can use moon water for watering plants to boost growth, charging crystals, enhancing baths or beauty rituals, and sprinkling around your space for protection or manifestation.

✦ ✦ ✦

MONEY RICE

Money money, money… okay I'll stop! Money rice is used to bring in prosperity, quick money, and abundance in all forms. It can be used to help with job interviews, reaching money goals, eradicating debt, and so much more. Anything money-related to be honest. So, if you're looking to spice up your money bowl or money rituals, money rice is the perfect way to do so. It's super simple and takes less than ten minutes to make. It's a good idea to pre-batch some, so you have it ready to go when needed.

What you'll need:

- A small bowl
- Uncooked rice (a money-drawing magnet)
- Green food coloring (to add to the prosperity vibes)
- Ground cinnamon (for fast success and prosperity)
- Dried basil (for attracting luck and financial success)

- Salt (for protecting your finances)
- An airtight container

What to do:

1. Start off by adding a few drops of food coloring to your rice and mix well. Make sure to stir clockwise to welcome in good fortune and prosperity. You can add a little more food coloring as you go along until you reach your desired color; just make sure not to add too much so the rice doesn't get soggy.

2. Next, add in your cinnamon, salt, and dried basil. These ingredients are going to be what gives your money rice that financial boost. As always, stir in your ingredients clockwise while focusing on your intentions to draw in your much-deserved wealth.

3. Once you've mixed everything together well, you're pretty much done! Store your money rice in an airtight container and place it on your altar for when you need it.

Witch Tip

Add a sprinkle of money rice to your wallet to manifest money on the go!

✦ ✦ ✦

HOW TO CREATE SIGILS

Sigils are symbols that can be created with specific intentions in mind. They can be used in pretty much any spell and for any intention. They can be carved into candles, put inside spell jars, or drawn on your body as a constant visual reminder of what you're manifesting. The easiest way to create a sigil is using the Austin Osman Spare method, which involves removing the vowels and duplicated letters from your written intention.

What to do:

1. Write out your intention in the present tense. For example, 'I am wealthy.'

2. Next, remove any vowels from your affirmation: A, E, I, O, U. For example, when you remove the vowels from 'I am wealthy,' you're left with 'M WLTHY'. If your intention has multiples of the same letter, remove any repeating letters, so that you end up with one of each.

3. Using the remaining letters, create a design that will become your sigil. Be as creative as you want – combine, overlap, or

stylize your sigil until it forms a unique design that feels powerful and symbolic to you.

4. Now energize your sigil by chanting, dancing, meditating with it, or leaving it out beneath the full moon. Whatever your gut is telling you to do, go with that!

5. Once you've created and charged your sigil, you're now free to use it however you see fit – for example, carving it into candles during spells, adding it to spell jars, or drawing it on your skin.

CORRESPONDENCE CHARTS

As promised, here are some quick reference charts for the herbs, candles, and crystals you may want to use in your spells. Knowing their spiritual meanings and properties will help guide you on how and when to incorporate them into your own spellwork.

Herbs and spices

Herb/spice	Spiritual meanings and properties
Allspice	Money, success, healing
Apples	Love, abundance, fertility
Basil	Love, abundance, good luck, money drawing
Bay leaves	Magick wishes, success, protection, prosperity
Black pepper	Banishing, protection, strength

Herb/spice	Spiritual meanings and properties
Calendula	Positivity, warmth, high vibrations
Catnip	Magnetisim, protection (against harm)
Chamomile	Relaxation, self-love, easing anxiety
Chili	Banishing, protection, passion, power
Cinnamon	Prosperity, good luck, abundance
Clove	Protection, clarity, attracting luck
Coffee	Energizing, revitalizing, focus
Coriander/Cilantro	Love, peace, health, fertility
Garlic	Protection, banishing evil, good health
Ginger	Power, passion, speed, protection
Lavender	Healing, peace, tranquility
Lemon	Cleansing, revitalizing, healing
Lime	Protection, purification, boundaries, prosperity
Mint	Prosperity, cleansing, communication, healing
Mugwort	Intuition, psychic enhancement, protection (especially psychic or spiritual), truth seeking
Nutmeg	Luck, money, legal success
Onion	Protection, truth, banishing

Herb/spice	Spiritual meanings and properties
Orange	Happiness, joy, uplifting energy
Paprika	Vitality, fire element boost, passion
Rose petals	Love, attraction, beauty, healing, emotional balance
Rosemary	Protection, clarity, healing
Sage	Knowledge, cleansing, protection
Salt	Protection, purity, banishing negativity
Thyme	Courage, purification, healing
Turmeric	Healing, prosperity, justice
Vanilla	Love, comfort, sensuality

Candle colors

Candle color	Spiritual meanings
Black	Banishing, protection, absorbing negative energy
Blue	Communication, truth revealing, peace and tranquility
Brown	Grounding, home stability, connecting to earth and ancestors
Gold	Success, abundance, masculine energy

Candle color	Spiritual meanings
Green	Good luck, money, growth, prosperity
Orange	Creativity, confidence, motivation
Pink	Love, friendship, healing
Purple	Intuition, psychic abilities, spiritual power, divination
Red	Passion, love, courage, strength
Silver	Moon energy, feminine divine, intuition, dream work
White	Cleansing, purification, and can represent any colored candle
Yellow	Joy, optimism, happiness

Crystals

Crystal	Spiritual meanings
Amethyst	Psychic protection, dream work, healing, calming
Citrine	Manifestation, abundance, joy, confidence
Clear quartz	Amplification, clarity, cleansing, programming intentions
Fluorite	Mental clarity, focus, healing
Malachite	Emotional healing, protection, prosperity

Crystal	**Spiritual meanings**
Moldavite	Transformation, spiritual awakening, rapid change
Obsidian	Protection, grounding, shadow work
Pyrite	Increasing net worth, positivity
Rose quartz	Self-love, romantic love, emotional healing
Tiger's eye	Confidence, protection, abundance

RUNES

Runes aren't just symbols, they're loud, ancient energy. Each one carries its own vibe, its own story. Use this chart to get to know them, feel them out, and pick the ones that align with whatever you're working on.

Rune	Name	Meanings
ᚠ	Fehu	Wealth, abundance, prosperity, new beginnings
ᚢ	Uruz	Strength, health, vitality, raw primal power
ᚦ	Thurisaz	Protection, conflict, challenges, defensive force
ᚨ	Ansuz	Communication, wisdom, divine messages, inspiration
ᚱ	Raidho	Travel, journey, life path, rhythm, movement

Rune	Name	Meanings
ᚲ	Kenaz	Knowledge, creativity, vision, illumination
ᚷ	Gebo	Gift, generosity, partnership, exchange, balance
ᚹ	Wunjo	Joy, harmony, success, emotional fulfillment
ᚺ	Hagalaz	Disruption, chaos, natural forces, necessary change
ᚾ	Nauthiz	Need, restriction, resistance, endurance, survival
ᛁ	Isa	Stillness, blockage, ice, pause, introspection
ᛃ	Jera	Harvest, reward, cycles, seasons, time and patience
ᛇ	Eiwaz	Transformation, death and rebirth, the yew tree, resilience
ᛈ	Perthro	Mystery, fate, secrets, the unknown, intuition
ᛉ	Algiz	Protection, higher self, guardianship, divine connection

Rune	Name	Meanings
ᛊ	Sowilo	Success, the sun, clarity, guidance, personal power
ᛏ	Tiwaz	Justice, honor, sacrifice, leadership, truth
ᛒ	Berkano	Birth, fertility, feminine energy, nurturing, growth
ᛖ	Ehwaz	Trust, movement, progress, loyalty, teamwork
ᛗ	Mannaz	The self, humanity, relationships, cooperation
ᛚ	Laguz	Emotions, intuition, water, flow, the unconscious
ᛜ	Ingwaz	Potential, inner power, gestation, completion
ᛞ	Dagaz	Breakthrough, awakening, clarity, transformation
ᛟ	Othala	Ancestry, inheritance, heritage, legacy, home

READING YOUR CANDLE FLAMES

When it comes to candle magick, being able to read your candle flames can give you an indication of how well your spell is working. Candle-flame reading is a form of divination known as pyromancy. It can help you to interpret messages from your own intuition, spirit guides, and any deities you may be working with.

Flame type	Meaning
Steady and strong	The spell is strong and is working exactly as you intended.
Flickering and dancing	Your spell is full of high energy, but it's also chaotic energy. Try to refocus your mind and intentions to ensure success.
High flame	Your spirit guides are backing your spell. It's likely to manifest quickly and easily. Just ensure your intentions are clear to avoid chaotic results.

Flame type	Meaning
Low and weak	Your spell is working, but you need to focus on your intentions more as there's currently something blocking your manifestations.
Popping or crackling	Your spirit guides are trying to send you a message. Pay attention to any thoughts that come to your mind, as these will give you an indication of the message. It could be a good sign or a sign of conflict, so listen to your gut instincts.
Smoking	Your spell is working, it's just facing some resistance. Try and home in on what that resistance is. A simple cleansing or banishing spell can help.
Multiple flames	Multiple energies are at play. This could either be your guide or a sign of conflict. Focus on your intentions as much as you can.

Sometimes when your candle shows these signs, it might not necessarily mean that energy is interfering with your spell. It could simply mean there's a bit of dirt or dust on your candle that's burning and causing your flame to act in a particular way. So, with any candle magick, ensure the wick is clean so that it can burn fully. If you're tying a piece of paper or a bay leaf to the stem of your candle, ensure you tie it low enough to prevent it from affecting your flame-reading results when you light the candle.

TIMINGS

Timing *isn't* everything – but it can boost your spellwork. You don't have to plan your spells by the moon phase or the day of the week, but syncing up your magick with the right moment can seriously amplify your results.

Timing	Association
New moon	New beginnings, setting new intentions, manifesting, starting projects, attraction
Waxing moon	Growth; healing; drawing in things such as money, love, and health
Full moon	Powerful manifestations, divination, charging tools
Waning moon	Releasing, banishing, letting go Spell intentions: cord cutting, breaking bad habits, protection

Timing	Association
Monday	Ruled by the Moon Spells relating to emotions, intuition, dreams, healing, fertility
Tuesday	Ruled by Mars Great for courage, protection, strength, conflict resolution
Wednesday	Ruled by Mercury Spell types: communication, travel, business, learning
Thursday	Ruled by Jupiter Great for abundance, luck, growth, success, expansion spells
Friday	Ruled by Venus Perfect for love, beauty, relationships, harmony spells
Saturday	Ruled by Saturn Great for banishing, boundaries, endings, justice, discipline
Sunday	Ruled by the Sun Perfect for boosting confidence, success, vitality, joy, goals

Timing	Association
Sunrise	New beginnings, energy, vitality Spells to start something or bring in hope
Noon	Clarity, power, success Good for confidence spells, goal setting, visibility
Sunset	Transition, balance, releasing Spells to let go, shift energy, break patterns
Midnight	Mystery, deep magic, spiritual work Good for divination, ancestor work, shadow work

A FINAL NOTE

Dear Reader,

Before I let you go, I just wanted to say this book was created for you – crafted with intention, love, and all the magick I could pour into these pages. It's more than just words; it's a guide, a companion, and a tool for your journey. I invite you to make it your own – scribble on the pages, doodle your symbols, and adapt the spells and recipes to fit your individual path. Turn these pages into your personal grimoire, a sacred space where your magick lives and grows.

Carry this book with you, pass it down through the generations, and let it become part of your altar, your rituals, and your daily practice. Use it as a reminder of your strength, your intuition, and your limitless ability to manifest the life you desire.

Your witchcraft journey is yours alone, but remember you are never truly alone. The witches who came before you, the universe that supports you, and this MysticPrimrose community stand beside you. This is your moment to rise, to claim your power, and to manifest like never before.

Now go forward with fierce confidence, knowing the magick is already within you. Trust your intuition, your own power, and never be afraid to be yourself. Your dream life is waiting – now is the time to manifest like the witch that you are. You're stronger than you think!

With all my love, light, and blessings,

Lilly

(aka MysticPrimrose)

ACKNOWLEDGMENTS

Bringing this book into the world has been a journey shaped by intuition, resilience, and a deep trust in the power of manifestation – even when the path didn't seem clear.

To my MysticPrimrose community – this truly wouldn't exist without you. Every order you've placed, every reel you've shared, every comment, like, message, and bit of love you've sent my way has helped breathe life into this book. You've supported my magick, my business, and my voice more than you'll ever know. You've shown me time and time again that this work matters. This book is my gift to you, for all your continuous love and support, this book is yours as much as it is mine.

To the witches who came before me – thank you for lighting the way. Your wisdom still whispers through the craft and lives in every spell, every page.

To my publisher, editor, and team – thank you for helping shape this with so much care and respect, and for honoring my truth through the entire process.

And to the universe – thank you for every nudge, sign, and bit of divine timing that reminded me to keep going, even when it felt impossible.

Let this book be your reminder:

You don't need permission to claim your power.

You are the spell. You are the fire.

And you can manifest anything – so stop doubting yourself and start owning the magick that already lives inside you. Your dream life is waiting for you.

With all my love and eternal gratitude,

Lilly

Photo by: Emma Griffin

About the Author

Lilly Statham is an influencer and serial entrepreneur celebrated for her profound expertise in witchcraft guidance and dynamic content creation. With a social media following of over 2.5 million people, Lilly's teachings empower others to manifest their dreams through the power of witchcraft. Lilly also runs a popular online witchcraft boutique Mystic Primrose, which has customers all over the world.

@MysticPrimrose

www.mysticprimrose.com

NOTES

We hope you enjoyed this Hay House book. If you'd like to receive our online catalog featuring additional information on Hay House books and products, or if you'd like to find out more about the Hay Foundation, please contact:

Hay House LLC, P.O. Box 5100, Carlsbad, CA 92018-5100
(760) 431-7695 or (800) 654-5126
www.hayhouse.com® • www.hayfoundation.org

Published in Australia by:
Hay House Australia Publishing Pty Ltd
18/36 Ralph St., Alexandria NSW 2015
Phone: +61 (02) 9669 4299
www.hayhouse.com.au

Published in the United Kingdom by:
Hay House UK Ltd
1st Floor, Crawford Corner,
91–93 Baker Street, London W1U 6QQ
Phone: +44 (0)20 3927 7290
www.hayhouse.co.uk

Published in India by:
Hay House Publishers (India) Pvt Ltd
Muskaan Complex, Plot No. 3,
B-2, Vasant Kunj, New Delhi 110 070
Phone: +91 11 41761620
www.hayhouse.co.in

CONNECT WITH

HAY HOUSE

ONLINE

hayhouse.co.uk

@hayhouse

@hayhouseuk

@hayhouseuk.bsky.social

@hayhouseuk

@HayHousePresents

Find out all about our latest books & card decks • Be the first to know about exclusive discounts • Interact with our authors in live broadcasts • Celebrate the cycle of the seasons with us • Watch free videos from your favourite authors • Connect with like-minded souls

'The gateways to wisdom and knowledge are always open.'

Louise Hay